PRAISE FOR *I CHOOSE ME*

. . . . .

"*I Choose Me* is for any women who is looking for more balance and fulfillment in every area of her life. Cynthia James offers practical tools, heartwarming stories, and powerful exercises that can help you experience radical self-care and mind/body nurturing. If you're ready to 'choose you,' this book is a must, and this is your time!"

Marci Shimoff, #1 NY Times bestselling author of
Happy for No Reason* and *Chicken Soup for the Woman's Soul

"Cynthia James is a force of nature. Throughout this beautiful book, Cynthia shares her profound insights, indomitable spirit and hard-won wisdom earned in the trenches of a troubled childhood. If you've ever been afraid that maybe you've been too hurt in life to turn it all around, reading this book will give you the courage and strength you need to come to a place of empowerment, peace and possibility. Hats off to this powerful woman for transforming her own life and then providing a powerful blueprint for how others might follow suit."

Katherine Woodward Thomas, NY Times Bestselling author of
Calling in "The One"

"Creating a big, fabulous, successful life is possible when you are willing to invest the time, energy, and resources necessary. And, if you are ready to get started right now, read this book by the brilliant and radiant Cynthia James. She shines a bright and clear light on the path to having it all."

Arielle Ford, author of *Turn Your Mate into Your Soulmate*

"Have you spent years putting everyone else first? Have you been taking care of people at work, at home and in your community, and there hasn't been any time or energy left for you? This book will change that. Cynthia shares powerful stories and strategies to help you step into the lead of your own life. Read it and reap."

Sam Horn, author of *"Got Your Attention?"*

"*I Choose Me* gives an inside view on how Cynthia James crafted a life of bold creativity, radiant spirituality and meaningful service. Through her life revelations, intimate stories and practical wisdom, she guides the reader toward their own unique expression, spiritual illumination and radical self-love."

Alexa Robbins, Professional Clairvoyant,
Movement Educator & Artist

"Cynthia has the gift of being a strong catalyst for meaningful shift into more awareness, deep healing, self-love, and making the bold move to our best yet-to-be. Her keen spiritual connection opens portals of insight and doors of opportunities we somehow missed! *I Choose Me* will prove to be a beloved companion for life's greater unfolding."

Donna DeNomme, Master Success Coach and Author of
Turtle Wisdom: Coming Home to Yourself* and *8 Keys to Wholeness:
Tools for Hope-Filled Healing

'Cynthia James is the spiritual big sister we all need and deserve. She's wise, powerful, and always ready to offer a shoulder to lean on and a hand up into a richer, more satisfying life! *I Choose Me* gives readers a chance to say yes to the lives where our contributions are priceless and our value profound. A must for every woman.'

Karen Russo, award winning author, *The Money Keys*
and *Grow Yourself, Grow Your Wealth*

"Out of the mud of an early life blooms the glorious lotus that is Cynthia James! Her gift of lifting and inspiring people, especially women, is truly extraordinary, whether you experience her across the table, in a workshop, or through her writings. She is a masterful teacher, a powerful guide, and a potent catalyst for transformation. Through story, penetrating insight, and spiritual alchemy, Cynthia weaves a tapestry of possibility that becomes a firm foundation from which to soar. She is a sister, a blessing, and a uniquely precious woman. Let her coach you into greater success than you ever dreamed possible."

Dr. Petra Weldes, Author *Joyous Living Journal, Joyous Freedom Journal*, and *Joyous Abundance Journal*

"Cynthia James is transforming lives across the planet, particularly women's lives, through her work and her words. *I Choose Me* has arrived at the perfect time, when I believe many of us are ready to step into our greater expression and live bigger lives. *I Choose Me* guides the reader toward greatness through Cynthia's sharing of personal stories and meditations, and by providing powerful questions, tools and action steps. Prepare to feed your soul and create the legacy you came here to live and to leave behind. Cynthia's passionate willingness to serve and step into her great big life shows up in *I Choose Me* and I am so glad she is sharing this powerful expression of her legacy."

Dr. Debra Rouse, Co-Author of *Think Eat Move: The Practice for an Awesome Life*

"No one delivers breakthrough tactics that WORK like Cynthia James. She helps us to find and refine our best self, and then leads us to launch our journey to its highest expression! Cynthia is your secret weapon for success!"

Betsy Wiersma, Founder of CampExperience™

"In the words of Cynthia James, 'there is no one path to peace and enlightenment.' In this book you will find a treasure trove of resources to begin building *your unique path* – one that will work for you. James' personal and revealing stories remind us that we are not alone. She helps us to remember that we have everything required to create the life we are meant to live. Don't delay. Get this book. Choose you!"

Marty Lassen, Principal, Complete Intelligence, LLC

"You are the most important person in your life." ...and with those words, Cynthia James captures the essence of self transformation. First deal with yourself, experience self compassion, build your accountability muscle...and then you can be present to the world, to be your best self, to step past fear toward a life fulfilled. Cynthia is a transformational leader who lays down the challenge, invites you to step up, and allows deep vulnerability... for that is where you hold your courage to live the life you want. *I Choose Me* is a beautiful blueprint, one you will return to again and again throughout your life.

Cheryl Esposito, CEO, Alexsa Consulting and Author,
In the Spirit of Leadership : A Vision Into A Different Future

Women continue to emerge as powerful entrepreneurs, wives, mothers and leaders. They are creating extraordinary new ways to run companies and express as way-showers in vast arenas. They are, however, grappling with how to care for self and live the life of their dreams. Cynthia James shows them how in this powerful book, *I Choose Me*. She shares heartwarming stories and gives practical tools for anyone in need of a more harmony and joy. This is a must read for any woman seeking the keys to choosing a more balanced life.

Justin Sachs, Best Selling Author of Innovative Women:
How the World's Top Female Entrepreneurs Make It Happen and
10 other best selling books on leadership and business success

I CHOOSE ME

**The *Art* of Being a Phenomenally
Successful Woman at Home and at Work**

CYNTHIA JAMES

Motivational PRESS
LEADERS IN GLOBAL PUBLISHING

Published by Motivational Press, Inc.
1777 Aurora Road
Melbourne, Florida, 32935
www.MotivationalPress.com

Manufactured in the United States of America.

ISBN: 978-1-62865-282-6

CONTENTS

* * * * *

YOUR HOME LIFE

CHAPTER ONE

CHAPTER TWO

CHAPTER THREE

YOUR WORK LIFE

CHAPTER FOUR

CHAPTER FIVE

YOUR INNER LIFE

CHAPTER THIRTEEN

FINAL THOUGHTS

DEDICATION

This book is dedicated to my beautiful female ancestors. Your brilliance, caring and courageous acts taught me to try and dare to shine my light. I also want to give great thanks to every woman who has ever dreamed big, dared to leap when she was afraid, or shown us that nothing is impossible. The women today stand on the shoulders of your bravery and vulnerability.

FOREWORD

* * * * *

Up until five years ago, I always put others ahead of myself at all costs. It was what I knew, being raised as a woman, and living as someone who was culturally sensitive, always tuned into others. And then tragedy stuck and I lost my brother and father and endured the end of my marriage. I realized I was out of integrity with the principles I taught. It was time to *Choose Me*.

If we are stripped, we have less to offer everyone else. *I Choose Me* is a courageous and really empowered choice, not just for ourselves as women, but for the world. We are the ones who make the heart-to-heart connections with other human beings and evolve our world together. We help love override fear, defensiveness and suspicion...one person at a time. We can love from a genuine place rather than loving to get something back. *I Choose Me* is the most important, honest, authentic and transformative choice we can make for ourselves to positively impact the world.

Self-love, checking in with yourself and taking care of your personal needs are monumental shifts that take a great deal of intention and courage because you will fight internal and social conditioning that says, as a woman, you should put others ahead of yourself. Trust me, I know. *Choosing Me* meant giving up everything I had built over three decades in Chicago and starting anew in Paris. It was there that I shared a powerful *Choose Me* moment with Cynthia James.

Cynthia quickly became a personal inspiration in my life, standing and praying with me when I first moved to Paris and helping me transition into my new home with peace and forgiveness. The first thing I noticed was her grounded and centered radiance. She is a powerful force of healing. When she speaks, it has a deep impact because she is speaking from a place of truth. She has seen the worst of life and has chosen to live with the highest ideals instead of being beaten down. Having seen every shade of life there is—from the darkest dark to the lightest light—she understands pain, suffering, fear and disappointment. Leading from personal experience makes her a tremendous guide, and what she offers is reliable and grounded.

Wherever you are, she will help you find your way to an empowered state of life. You can feel assured in investing in her because she knows what it is to *Choose Me* when the whole world says you can't, and she is well-versed in helping others do the same.

I had the good fortune of sharing time with Cynthia, her husband and her granddaughter in Paris, and was witness to her laying the foundation for the next generation through her devotion. She is leaving a huge legacy and a tsunami-size shift in everyone she touches. This is her gift to all of us, after she has faced the worst and created the best. Her presence and work has a vibration that awakens that possibility within each of us. I saw that in being with her and her granddaughter.

Her devotion to emancipation from helping women from their own undoing is unsurpassed. She will show you, step by step, how to create a new foundation and empower and teach you how to feed yourself the spiritual food you need. She understands that it is about more than ideals: it is about decisions. If you choose to show up, she will show you the way to love and truly empowered living.

The fact that you've found your way to this book means you're ready, and you couldn't be in better hands. This is not just a work about what we should do, but what we can do. You will experience words, a presence and a consciousness that will activate an energy within you, as Cynthia guides you to make shifts in your life. And that's where the real magic happens.

You can trust her words because she's telling the truth. You'll feel it in your cells. Cynthia James is a truly gifted leader who will lead you back to the best of you. She did it for me, and I'm certain she will help do the same for you.

Now is your time. Choose *I Choose Me* and make the most courageous choice you can make as a human being, and woman, today.

—Sonia Choquette, New York Times Bestselling Author

INTRODUCTION

· · · · ·

I have always been a dreamer. I have always wondered outside the "box" of my circumstances and opened to creating a world of beauty and fulfillment. As a very young child, I dreamed of traveling the world and living a life of luxury and adventure.

I remember being four years old and pretending to be a singer, dancer and actress. I dressed up in my mother's clothes. I put on shows for anyone who was around me. I recruited my cousins to create shows and dance theatre performances. I watched movies and imagined myself being a star.

Somehow, it never dawned on me that those dreams couldn't come true because everyone in my family believed that choices were minimal. The spoken and unspoken message was that we were victims of a society that was filled with struggle and sacrifice. Couple that with the fact that the majority of women surrounding me were beautiful, brilliant and creative, but believed they had no skills or understanding because they lived in a world of infinite possibilities. So, my dreams seemed outrageous.

I saw and experienced a lot of violence and trauma in my youth. My alcoholic father floated in and out of my life until he died when I was fourteen. My stepfather consistently beat my mom and molested me. I lived in constant fear of being awakened by my mother's screams or being dragged into a room where cries for help were inconsequential. We finally escaped when my uncle rescued us in the one hour that my stepfather and sister were out of the house. We put all of our belongings in sheets and jumped in the car. I was six years old.

Although I didn't feel safe, I refused to let the victim feelings that permeated my family deter me from believing that I could make my dreams come true. I refused to give up and accept that the current reality was destined to be my life. Something in me knew I could be more. Even when my family members called me a dreamer and "fantasy girl," I simply said to myself, "they have no idea who I will become."

In school, I began to notice that many of the girls lacked vision. They wanted to play house and be mothers or pretend to be nurses. I wanted to be an artist and performer so that I could fulfill my dreams of traveling. I didn't understand enculturation or the fact that historically women had been told, on many levels, that we had a role in society and should not try to move outside the norms of what was expected. I was aware that many of my teachers and caregivers not so subtly reminded me that girls were not doctors, entrepreneurs, pilots or business people. Our job was to get married and care for our families. I would ask "why?" and was told to be a "good girl."

Let me share a little history here. In the eighteenth century, especially in marriage, men were taught to rule over their wives. Women were property and belonged to the husband. Men were the primary breadwinners and, if a woman worked, her employment was primarily low status, low paid, and involved fewer skills and responsibilities than a man's. The focus of the type of work available to women was as an extension of women's home responsibilities, such as domestic service, teaching and nursing. Women in public roles were asked to stay focused on their moral and domesticated virtues by participating in religion and charity.

In 1873, Edward Clarke, a doctor and former professor at Harvard Medical School, wrote his reasons why women should not be educated, and published them in his book, *Sex in Education; Or, A Fair Chance for The Girls*. He believed that women were predestined to be propagators of the human race. Therefore, education was of secondary importance.

He pointed out that their brains were inferior to men's, and thus weren't meant to handle higher levels of education.

There is also a quote from Martin Luther: "Girls begin to talk and to stand on their feet sooner than boys because weeds always grow up more quickly than good crops."

Even though highly skilled and professional women moved to the forefront in the 1900's, that misguided energy and those spoken and unspoken beliefs bombarded me well into my twenties. Let me say here—for any of you who were born with a rebellious nature—those conversations became a catalyst for me to break the rules and push the walls of my current reality. I knew I was poor, stood in welfare lines and wore hand-me-down clothes. The women in my family all worked in jobs they hated, but I was clear that my life was destined for another path. A personal drive developed that was powerful and relentless. I was clear that this current lifestyle was not my destiny.

In high school, I stepped out in a big way. I joined the debate and chess clubs. I took French and Latin. I sang in the high school choir and became a soloist in talent shows. I was also selected as a teen model in a large department store. In my junior year, I joined an all-male band, and we traveled throughout the state of Minnesota; even to Colorado. I moved out of my family's home in my senior year and shared an apartment with four other girls. My mother was terrified that I was throwing my life away. However, during that time, I maintained an "A" average, became the secretary of my class, and was voted "most talented." I was determined to live a life that was rich and full.

Many of the girls I grew up with had multiple failed relationships; some had illegitimate children and some experienced drug challenges. The interesting thing is that these girls were beautiful, smart and had big dreams. What they didn't have were powerful models and mentors who could encourage them to follow their passions.

My life unfolded and I went on to become successful, singing internationally, working as an actress in television and film, authoring several books, and coaching people to live powerful and productive lives. Today, I understand that, even as a child, on some level I was called to create an expansive life and to model possibility for others.

This book is for any woman who wants to live a bigger life. It is for you if you are feeling a call to bring your voice to the world, your community, your relationships or your career. The women we admire today got to where they are because they had a vision; they activated creativity, up-leveled their skillsets and dared to be bold. They are not the exception—they are the example.

Here are a few of the women I admire:

Carole Black – President and CEO of Lifetime Entertainment Services.

Oprah Winfrey – Host of the nation's best-rated talk show for sixteen years and head of Harpo Inc., which generated spin-off products such as *O, The Oprah Magazine* and the OWN network.

Margaret C. Whitman – Internet entrepreneur who transformed eBay, Inc., from a web-based flea market to a global merchandising force with $13 billion in sales.

Madame C. J. Walker – entrepreneur who established a lucrative cosmetics company that makes beauty products for African American consumers.

Meryl Streep – A great actress known for her brilliance, excellence and authenticity.

Lisa Nichols – Bestselling author and CEO of Motivating the Masses.

Serena Williams – One of the greatest tennis players of all time.

Each of these women focused on her vision, overcame obstacles and dared to shine her light. As I reflect on my admiration for them, I can see that they, by example, have invited me/us to step up, step out and remind the world that our presence on this planet is necessary and essential.

HOW TO USE THIS BOOK:

· · · · ·

There are three sections to this book: Your Home Life, Your Work Life and Your Inner Life, all addressing the biggest arenas for growth. Each chapter has insights and revelations from my own journey, and exercises to support you in moving to your next level of creating a life that is fulfilling and joyous. We have all experienced how easy it is to get distracted, so each exercise is specifically designed to keep you focused and on target. Also, each chapter includes a story or two written by one of the women who have worked with me to create the life of their dreams.

Have you ever wondered why you keep making the same mistakes or critical judgments? Have you ever wondered if you are going to get out of your rut and start thriving? I believe that your greatest work is to commit. Commit to yourself. Commit to the dream that wants to be realized as *you*. Commit to moving forward, even when you are frightened. Commit because you have a message that no one else can deliver in the way that you can.

In a 2015 article in *MORE Magazine,* Michelle Obama and Meryl Streep had a beautiful conversation about being a woman today. Both women were asked what legacy they wanted to leave. This is what they shared:

Michelle: "I want to feel like the things I did made a difference...I am always thinking maybe this interaction, particularly if I am meeting kids, will change someone's life. That's how I think about the work I do [as First Lady). It is a rare spotlight. I want to make sure I don't waste it."

Meryl: "But when I think about what I really want to leave behind, I realize it's what my mother left me. For the people that I touched and cared about, I want it to matter to them that I was in their lives."

A few years ago, I sat with Lisa Nichols and she asked a question about the legacy I wanted to leave. It was a moment of great transformation and, quite frankly, I was scared. She looked me in the eyes and said, "You are here to make a difference. What is your legacy? How do you want to be remembered?" In that moment, my heart opened and my answer led me on an amazing journey of discovery and expansion.

It is my deep desire that this book supports you in revealing and creating your legacy. I know you are here to make a difference and deliver your message in your way. The portal to delivering that message is in the answer to the question: WHAT IS YOUR LEGACY?

YOUR HOME LIFE

This section focuses on your personal life. It includes self-care, creating conscious intimate relations and becoming a powerful parent. It is said that home is where the heart is. Use this information to nurture your heart and your connection with yourself and others.

CHAPTER ONE

ESTABLISHING HEALTH AND INTIMACY IN RELATIONSHIPS

. . . . .

To be yourself in a world that is constantly trying to make you something else is the greatest accomplishment.

—Ralph Waldo Emerson

Relationships have been a path of discovery for me. It took me many years to create a loving marriage and partnership, and that only happened after years of frustration, betrayal and abandonment. Let me be clear: I have dated, married and had momentary encounters with the same man in a different body numerous times. What I mean by that is that they have all had the same challenges in life, and they all mirrored the parental figures from my childhood. They had addictive personalities and were often abusive and unkind. I gave my power away each time, hoping that I could get the love that I did not get as a child. If there was one dysfunctional man in the room, I was drawn to him like a magnet. Today, I understand that they were all here for my healing but, during those difficult years, I couldn't see beyond the pain that was occurring in those relationships.

I once went to a psychic, hoping to get some support. She said, "Why are you here?" I told her I wanted to find my soul mate and get married. She smiled and said, "No you don't. If you wanted that, you would already have it." She then looked me in the eyes and said, "The image I see with you is that you are on a path with a big boulder in front of you. You are struggling to get over the boulder, and it never dawns on you that you can just walk around it to continue on the path." I didn't totally get it at the time but, today, I can see that the moment I stopped searching, my beloved husband appeared.

I often support couples in my practice, and they almost always come in to fix something they perceive as wrong in the relationship. Here is what I love to say to them: "What if there is nothing wrong with your relationship? What if you are here to recognize and reveal your own defenses, insecurities and need to control? What if those discoveries are a portal to true intimacy and connection?"

They often look at me with confusion in their eyes. How can there be nothing wrong? Why else would we be here? That is the $100,000,000 question. The answer, actually, lives in the question.

Every relationship is nothing but a mirror: they all tell you how successful you are at being with yourself. It doesn't matter if it is in your biological familial dynamics, business environment or relationships with children or friends. It all comes down to you being willing to take a deep, hard look at yourself.

Here is the truth: we all want to be seen, heard, understood and loved. Where we get confused is that this level of connection is an inside job. If you want to be honored, honor yourself. If you want to be in integrity-filled relationships, be in integrity with yourself. You will never be happy with anyone else, on any level, if you are not happy with yourself.

THE SOUL MATE YOU ARE SEEKING IS YOU

I believe we are all here to discover the deep essence of loving that lives within us. We get fooled into thinking that some magical, mystical person is going to show up and bring happiness into our lives. We search and we search. We kiss a lot of frogs, hoping they will turn into a prince or princess. When that doesn't work, we find ourselves spiraling down into a never-ending pit of self-pity, self-doubt, self-condemnation and judgment of ourselves and of others.

Being human is fascinating. It has so many of us looking for love anywhere and everywhere. Sometimes, that looking creates non-supportive relationships. We know intellectually that we need to love ourselves first, but we are convinced, internally, that if we get it from the outside, life will be good. The interesting thing about that belief is that all people have character flaws and moments of being unconscious. When we put all of our dreams of love and validation into the hands of another person, we are frequently disappointed. It can look like betrayal, inconsiderate behavior, and lack of interest or emotional misconduct. We take these actions on as "wounds", and begin to create beliefs about our unworthiness or inability to attract love.

Here is what I would like you to think about: are you treating yourself the way you want to be treated? Are you honoring and respecting yourself, and asking others to do the same? Are you caring for the temple that is your body? Are you presenting your best self every time you leave your house? Are you being the love that you desire? What would your life be like if you loved yourself so deeply that the world had no choice but to love you back?

Tina Turner sang the successful song, "What's Love Got to Do with It?" Basically, she was saying: "why have a heart and open it when a heart can be broken?" In a way, I understand that feeling. A lot of us have had our hearts broken more than once, but here is the thing: you are not broken. You are lovable because you exist. I do not believe that some-one has to deliver you flowers, candy or a card to validate your amazing beauty and life. You have within you gifts that cannot be measured. You are unique, creative, powerful, talented and loving. I say, "Begin by loving yourself." It is time to make you the number one priority. Nurture yourself. Be kind to yourself. Trust yourself. Respect yourself. Use meditation as a tool to reconnect to your spirit. A consistent spiritual practice will bring you to a remembrance that you have always been loved and important.

I believe that:

» Love is all around us.

» Love is the essence of the Spirit.

» Every act of loving kindness is a reflection of the infinite Love that is available.

» Love flows from within and is not something that you get.

Open to loving yourself and witness how important you are in this world.

What's love got to do with it? EVERYTHING! Love is who you are.

Conscious coupling takes practice

I have been with my husband for 22 years. We have been married for almost 18 of those years. Before this relationship, I was unable to be in a sustainable partnership. It finally dawned on me that I was the common denominator in all of my failed connections and, if I was going to have a lasting relationship, I had to do some work on me. I did just that, and Carl appeared in my life. That is the good news. The interesting news is that we both discovered that our work was just beginning. Neither of us had a model for healthy relationships. We both had gone through painful divorces and challenges in partnering. So, the question became, "How can we do this differently?"

The fantasy person inside of me wanted the love to be enough. I knew better, since that had not proven to be true in the past. There is a powerful soul recognition with my husband, and we share many common interests. He is a man dedicated to spiritual growth, and that was important to me. He comes from a Jewish heritage and a deeply intellectual family. They are very devoted to one another, and that was a big plus for me. My African American roots were fiery and emotion-based. The differences in our backgrounds proved to be fertile soil for healing, loving and growth.

We are both independent souls, and that supported our commitment to self -expression. I was clear that I did not want to give my power away and become a reflection of *his* great desires. I had done that many times, and it did not work. The question became, "how do I stand in my personal power and be a loving, giving wife?" Asking that question proved to be the foundation for the practice of conscious loving.

At first, the fact that I wanted to fight for my voice in the relationship only caused more fighting. Then, I pulled back my voice to create peace. That caused internal resentment and anger. Finally, I decided to commit to speaking my truth, asking for what I needed and expecting that my husband loved me enough to hear me. Wow! What a journey. I had never been that vulnerable, and it was scary. I cannot say it has been easy, but that consistent practice of being present has been a powerful and deep expansion of soul commitment in my marriage.

THE NEED TO PROCESS

I was sitting with a client, and we were discussing his current relationship. He was concerned about the differences in their communication styles and the inability to find ways to be heard. I asked what they were doing to gain clarity. He said, "Well, we talk about everything and try to find a solution." I asked, "How is that working?"

He smiled and told me that they just got deeper into the challenge and sometimes needed space from each other. I looked at him and asked, "What if there is nothing to fix?" He was perplexed.

I continued. "What is the need you have to process everything? You are looking for what is wrong, finding it, and then trying to fix it. Sounds exhausting to me." Our work continued in this area for several sessions. The root of the challenge was that both people were afraid to fail, and so they were "working" to get it right.

Have you ever seen that picture where you could see the image of either an old woman or a beautiful young woman? Once you are shown a different way of looking at the picture, the image shifts. What you see depends on your perspective. The same is true of life. The way that you see your life today is through a filter of your experiences, beliefs and patterns. Some perspectives are conscious, and others live in the unconscious. Unconscious beliefs can color your life expressions without you being aware that they exist. These beliefs are energetic magnets that move into the field of life, find their energetic match, and then re-create them in the form of our lives.

FIND ANOTHER VIEWPOINT

Many of us on the planet are baby boomers. Some of us are aging with vitality, joy, enthusiasm and grace. Others are struggling, feeling unhealthy and consistently resisting the natural changes in life. What is the difference? Perspective and choice! You are a powerful manifestation of divine intelligence. That means that you are equipped with everything you need to live a fulfilled life. If that is not your experience in this moment, change your point of view. Look at life and your relationships from another viewpoint. Choose to release old barriers and call forth grace. Ask for assistance in seeing with fresh eyes. You are surrounded by a generous, loving presence that wants to support your greatness. Open now and see the new you. Your relationships do not have to be hard.

COMMUNICATION EXERCISES

• • • • •

COMMUNICATION OF FEELINGS

Walls are illusions! These walls are opportunities to know yourself and your partner better. They are opportunities to grow individually and collectively. This is a chance to go deeper in your love. When challenges arise (because they will), ask the following questions:

» How do I feel?

» What do I want?

» How is my past coloring my present?

» What am I getting out of staying stuck?

» What do I need to say?

» What agreements have I broken?

» Am I making the other person wrong?

» Am I trying to control my partner or this situation?

» Where have I withheld the truth or my love?

» How can I be of service to this relationship and myself?

MIRROR TECHNIQUE

Tell your partner the message you would like him or her to hear and understand. The message should start with "I" and describe your feelings. (Example: "I feel hurt when you yell at me," or "I shut down when I don't feel heard.")

» Your partner then mirrors your message. Example: "If I heard you correctly, you feel hurt when I yell at you. Is that accurate?"

» If you feel your partner didn't fully understand your message, explain again and have them mirror you until the message is received.

If you were heard accurately, your partner says, "Is there more about that?" This helps you complete your feelings and prevents your partner from responding to incomplete messages.

When the message is completed, the partner then summarizes all of the message. (Example: "Let me see if I understood it all, I heard...")

Once the PARTNER is clear, they offer a different approach:

"So, in the future, it would be more supportive of our relationship if I..."

FIRST PARTNER responds in the positive.

AFTER THE MIRROR EXERCISE

First partner acknowledges being heard and understood, and appreciates partner for being willing to participate.

It is important for each person to honor the process and keep any agreements made. It can take some time to become proficient. Habits can be hard to break. Willingness to change is the key.

AFFIRMATION

You can read this daily to anchor embracing deep and powerful love in your life.

Today, I stand in the awareness that I am deeply and powerfully loved. I am supported in extraordinary ways because I exist. I am an expression of love made manifest. My relationships mirror this truth in ways I could not have imagined. I treat myself the way I want to be treated. I expect and demand that others treat me the same way. I open my heart and expect authentic, loving relationships to come to me. I am 100% clear that love will not elude me.

RECLAIMING THE PARTS OF MYSELF I HAD DISOWNED

. . . . .

—Angela Sasseville, MA, LPC

In the early years of our marriage, my husband must have thought that he had married a crazy person. After a long day at work as our sole breadwinner, he would announce that he was headed out on a mountain bike ride. I knew that cycling was his passion, so the strong, independent and capable side of me would supportively reply, "Oh, honey. That's a great idea. Have a nice ride. I'll hang out at home with the baby until you get back."

Hours would pass. I never knew when to expect him back. Still trying to cling to the autonomy that he had before our marriage, he refused to commit to a time. I'd been home alone with the baby all day while studying for graduate school, and my parenting muscles, along with my patience, would wear out. The baby would become cranky and I would become overwhelmed and stressed, trying to cook dinner with a fussy child on my hip.

As the evening wore on, the strong and independent side of me would take leave of my body. What would materialize in its place was a part of me I had disowned long ago, a part of me whose needs had *never* been met in my primary relationships. It was a part of me that was *not* super woman and that did, in fact, have her own breaking points and needed support. That part of me felt alone and stretched thin.

I judged this emerging part of me as "needy", and I felt ashamed of it. It is my *interdependent* side that has an undeniable need for the connection and support of another like I need air to breath. That part of me was emerging and was no longer willing to be ignored, but I was resistant to admitting that side of me existed. I didn't want to be reliant on attention and engagement from my husband in order to feel happy and secure in our marriage.

My interdependent side had been waiting in the shadows, unseen and unacknowledged, since I was a little girl. Ignoring it and showing up as strong and independent instead was a survival strategy I developed to cope in my family. My father was an emotionally unavailable workaholic. He was ignorant of my need for his attention and clueless to the pain that his chronic lack of involvement caused me.

After years of receiving reinforcing messages that it was better to be strong and independent, I was uncomfortable being vulnerable and reliant upon others. I had yet to learn how to integrate that part of me or advocate for my interdependent needs so that I could be whole.

My husband received the mixed messages that came from the two sides of me, wrestling one another for control. He resented my inconsistency. Upon his return from his bike ride, I greeted my husband not with warmth but with coldness. He felt set up. How could I dare be angry about something that I had cheerfully granted him permission to do just hours earlier? It was crazy-making to him, and I didn't understand it at the time, either. I'd greet him with anger and he'd get defensive and quickly shut down. This was the dance we both engaged in any time there was conflict.

I would later realize that it wasn't my husband's long physical absences during his bike rides that were the sole problem for me: his absences were compounded by his emotional unavailability when he was at home. The quantity of our time together wasn't the real issue: we lacked quality time together.

Time passed, and the dynamics between us didn't improve. On the darkest night of my marriage, I sat down at the computer and typed up an Excel spreadsheet of what my household budget would look like if I left my husband and attempted to support our children as a single parent. The business that I own was in its infancy then, and wasn't very profitable. The spreadsheet confirmed my suspicions. The numbers didn't add up, and there was no obvious way in which ending my marriage was going to be financially workable.

Yet in that moment, I made a conscious decision to choose me. I reclaimed my vulnerable and neglected interdependent side as a valid and integral part of my whole. I insisted that my need for support and connection would no longer be denied me.

I committed to myself that, unlike so many women I had witnessed who live out entire lifetimes playing small in unhappy relationships, I would *not* stay in an unfulfilling marriage simply because I was afraid that my financial needs would not be met.

I announced to my husband that if he was not interested in learning how to change his behavior to meet my needs, our journey together would soon end. Despite the enormous fear that I had about losing him, I had to stand in the truth that, although I can be strong and independent, I also deserved to collapse into the arms of a lover at the end of a hard week. I had to claim my right to be interdependent upon someone, and to be nurtured and supported.

As I insisted that my needs be met *no matter what the cost,* my husband finally awakened from the disengaged stupor he'd been living in. He didn't want to lose me, but he wasn't happy. I wasn't meeting *his* emotional needs, either. So, instead of just soldiering through more of the status quo that *wasn't* serving him, as men so often do, he had to become more self-aware so he could identify and communicate what *he* needed from me. I, too, had to change my behavior to make space for his needs.

In relationships of the highest vibrational frequency, *both* partners thrive emotionally. They have both reclaimed their disowned parts and have become whole. It's this wholeness that allows them to be truly seen and nurtured by one another.

CHAPTER TWO

SELF-CARE IS NON-NEGOTIABLE

• • • • •

Knowing how to be solitary is central to the art of loving. When we can be alone we can be with others without using them as a means of escape.

—Bell Hooks

Often we lose our identity trying to please or placate others.

—Mary Manin Morrissey

I love to perform. No matter where I am or what I am doing, I create a way to let my "artist in residence" find a way to express itself. I was working in corporate communications and producing executive events for the company that employed me. It was hectic and oftentimes stressful. At the same time, I was choreographing Romeo and Juliet for Deaf West, a theatre company producing plays with deaf actors. It was exhilarating. Romeo was deaf and Juliet was not. I was high on the opportunity to stretch as an artist and get to work with amazing actors.

I would go to work at 7 a.m., work until 6 p.m., and then make my way to the theater. This went on for four weeks of rehearsals, one week of previews and an opening to a lovely reception by the public. I was ecstatic.

One morning, a few weeks later, I woke up and knew I had a full day at work. I am a morning person, so I was filled with ideas about how the day should unfold. I got out of bed and fell on the floor. I could not walk. My husband got up and tried to help me stand. No way. I immediately got scared and we made a doctor's appointment. They told me that I had strained a muscle and gave me muscle relaxers. That did nothing but make me unfocused and woozy. So, I decided to grin and bear it. I slowly began to walk, but it was painful, and I still had no clue why this was happening.

My husband's family was connected to a chiropractor through marriage. We were at a family gathering and I explained my situation. The doctor said, "Come and see me. Maybe I can help." Anything was worth a try, so I went in a couple of days later. In less than five minutes he told me that I had a torn *psoas*. That is the muscle that helps you lift your leg. He explained that the problem was due to overtaxing the muscle, probably done while I was greatly fatigued and unaware of the pressure I was putting on that area of my body.

That was a pivotal moment. I knew I had been pushing my body. I knew I was not getting enough rest or eating well. I knew I was committed to impressing the director and actors with my skill. I knew that my daily meditation practice was suffering as well and, I knew, without a shadow of a doubt, that I was ignoring signs that I needed to take care of myself.

YOU ARE THE MOST IMPORTANT PERSON IN YOUR LIFE

Most of us have not been trained to understand that we must come first. We are often shamed or made to feel guilty if we don't take care of others before we meet our needs. We drop whatever we are doing to make an impression on our boss or be so important that people cannot do without us.

When I was moving from California to Colorado, my children were upset. I knew I had a "calling," and moving was imperative. However, I was plagued wondering if my children would ever forgive me for leaving them. I complained to a friend, and finally she said, "Now they will have to learn to take care of themselves." I instantly went into defending how I had raised them, and how much they needed my support. She simply smiled and said, "Or you could have been enabling them to depend on you." Yuck; that stung with great elements of truth.

PEOPLE WILL ALWAYS FIND A WAY

I was so arrogant; I actually believed that my children, my friends and family members needed me to be the "one." Here is the interesting thing: when I moved to Colorado, my kids bonded in a new way and began to take care of each other. My friends found new places and experiences to support them. I had elected myself the organizer of all events and, when I left, someone else took my place. Even though all of that was true, I still didn't get it. I moved into full-time ministry. I gave my all to making a difference. I worked 50-60 hours a week. It was fulfilling, but I, once again, forgot to take care of me first.

I gained 30 pounds. I overtaxed my adrenals and the stress drove my blood pressure up. I told myself that I knew what to do and, as soon as I got a chance, I would implement a good self-care plan.

When my body began to shut down again and I had to take a sabbatical, the world did not stop because I wasn't there. I knew that what I contributed had value, but there were others ready and willing to step in and support the areas I managed. During that sabbatical, I came to some powerful revelations.

EXERCISE IS MY FRIEND

There is overwhelming scientific evidence that we NEED to exercise to be healthy. It supports healthy metabolism, focuses the mind, strengthens our bones, anchors healthy weight and nurtures our immune system. So, why do so many people find excuses not to exercise?

Here are some startling statistics on *exercise* from the President's Council on Fitness, Sports & Nutrition:

» Fewer than 5% of adults participate in 30 minutes of physical activity each day; only one in three adults pursues the recommended amount of physical activity each week.

» Only 35–44% of adults 75 years or older are physically active, and only 28-34% of adults ages 65-74 are physically active.

» More than 80% of adults do not meet the guidelines for both aerobic and muscle-strengthening activities, and more than 80% of adolescents do not do enough aerobic physical activity to meet the guidelines for youth.

» Children now spend more than seven and a half hours a day in front of a screen (e.g., TV, videogames, computer).

» 28% of Americans, or 80.2 million people, aged six and older, are physically inactive.

I don't know about you, but secretly I believed that my body would support my insane behavior forever. I never stopped to think about the fact that every aspect of nature requires rest, some form of nurturing and healthy nutrition.

One day, I was at a resort and there were signs around saying not to feed the animals. I was reading a sign and a caretaker came by. I asked why it was dangerous to feed the animals. He smiled and said, "Most people don't ask. They think they are being nice. To name a few:

» Human food is not made for animals. It can cause disease and even death.

» Feeding an animal changes its normal behavior.

» Feeding wildlife can make them dependent on humans as a source of food and they may become unable to survive on their own."

He then smiled and walked away. I stood for a moment, and then I thought, "I wonder how much I am consuming that is unhealthy for my life or not *meant for human consumption?*"

RECHARGE THROUGH NUTRITION

It is December, one of my busiest months, and I am exhausted. I get on the scale and see that 30 pounds has miraculously leaped onto my stomach and thighs. I knew I was gaining weight, but I am a creative dresser and covered it up with fabric and goddess clothes. It is amazing how easy it is to rationalize a lack of self-care. I was eating relatively healthy. I am a vegetarian and eat only fish as a protein additive, but I was completely unaware of how much of my eating was emotionally-based. I was not being honest with myself, and my body was showing me how the dishonesty was playing out.

» I paid no attention to portion control.

» I paid no attention to my consistent salt and sugar intake.

» I ate late at night after teaching.

» I relied on protein drinks and bars to curb hunger.

Here are some interesting statistics on *nutrition* from the President's Council on Fitness, Sports & Nutrition:

» Food safety awareness goes hand-in-hand with nutrition education. In the United States, food-borne agents affect one out of six
individuals and cause approximately 48 million illnesses; 128,000
hospitalizations; and 3,000 deaths each year.

» Typical American diets exceed the recommended intake levels or
limits in four categories: calories from solid fats and added sugars,
refined grains, sodium, and saturated fat.

» About 90% of Americans eat more sodium than is recommended
for a healthy diet.

» Reducing the sodium Americans eat by 1,200 mg per day could
save up to $20 billion a year in medical costs.

» Food consumption increased in all major food categories from
1970 to 2008. Average daily calories per person in the marketplace
increased approximately 600 calories.

» Since the 1970s, the number of fast food restaurants has more
than doubled.

» More than 23 million Americans, including 6.5 million children,
live in food deserts—areas that are more than a mile away from a
supermarket.

A PLAN IS ESSENTIAL

Anyone who knows me is clear that I am not a sports enthusiast.
However, I do love the incredible commitment and tenacity of athletes.
They have a plan and a coach to assist in implementing that plan. I knew
if I was going to change, I needed a plan. Even if I released the weight, I
needed to know how to stay on track.

I consulted a nutritionist and initiated a cleanse and an expansive
plan to stay focused. Today, I am 30 pounds lighter and have held that
weight for four years. I am including my "cleanse and clear" plan in this
book. It may not be the plan for you, but I really encourage you to do
something that is sustainable to help you stay focused on self-care.

SELF-CARE EXERCISES

· · · · ·

CLEANSE AND CLEAR PLAN

Tool #1: Activate the Witness

There is nothing to do here but simply step back and "see" how your behavior and patterns are showing up in the world. You are encouraged to journal through this process. It will be too difficult to remember everything without your documentation, and you really want to be clear about your patterns. It is important not to judge yourself or what you discover. You have an opportunity here to become totally awake to the call for your expansion. Here are the seven "activating your witness" steps.

1. "Witness" what you eat and how often you eat for comfort or distraction.

2. "Witness" what triggers you and how often it takes you to become overwhelmed.

3. "Witness" when you decide to skip or reduce your spiritual practice.

4. "Witness" your reluctance to self-nurture and care for yourself.

5. "Witness" your rationalizations for playing small and/or withholding your wisdom.

6. "Witness" any negative self-talk or desire to engage with others in gossip.

7. "Witness" when the need to control anything or anyone emerges and "how" it moves into action.

Tool #2: Invoke Visionary Contemplations

You can do these as a long spiritual practice or use one question at a time. It is important to give yourself time to be still and get quiet. If you can, do this in the same place every day. Make sure you have a journal or paper with you.

Sit down (you can have quiet music if it helps) and begin to breathe slowly. Breathe in, and breathe out. Some people find that watching the breath supports relaxation. If your mind is "chattering," it is fine. Don't resist, just put your attention on the breath and have it fill every area of your body until you begin to relax. Now, ask a question and just listen. Don't judge what comes. This is a non-linear process. Write down thoughts, feelings, colors, ideas, words or quotes. If you are only doing one question at a time, give thanks for the information and bless this process. If you are doing all of the questions, gently go back to the breath and ask the next question until you are complete. NOTE: This is not a practice to tell you what to do; it is a practice of opening to possibility.

QUESTIONS FOR CONTEMPLATION

» What is the highest vision for my life?

» What must be released to fulfill that vision? Example: patterns, fears, addictions, beliefs, etc.

» What makes my heart sing and smile? Example: passions, adventures, experiences, people, etc.

» Where can I be of service that makes a difference? (This is not a place where you are paid).

» Who are the people who inspire me and why? How am I like these people?

» Where are the places I have made a difference this year?

» If there were no obstacles, what would I be doing?

If you currently desire a change or are in transition, I suggest you do these contemplations for 30 days. Then, review your journal to support any important decisions. The 30 days will give time for you to embrace and embody the information that has been given. You might also notice that during the 30 days, answers and solutions may "drop" into your life without you doing anything.

Tool #3: Create a "Possibility Plan"

Here are some suggestions to support you in creating a plan that can work to help you expand into the life you desire. Use any or all of them.

1. *Find a cleanse program that resonates with you.* There are many. You want it to support you in cleansing out your body so that you can be more clear and focused. For some, "fasting" works. For others, gentle cleanse programs are more beneficial. It does not matter which one you choose. Just choose.

2. *Commit to some form of exercise.* Begin with two days a week. You can walk, go to a gym, follow a yoga tape or take a class. The important thing is to move your body. Once you start cleansing, emotional baggage will appear. Moving your body helps to release that old energy and makes room for revelations.

3. *Commit to a minimum of 5 minutes a day for spiritual practice.* Twenty minutes is ideal, but 5 minutes is a great place to start. I strongly suggest doing this first thing in the morning to jumpstart your day.

4. *Make a list of areas that need to be cleaned or reorganized.* Put the list in order of priority and do them one at a time. Be sure to celebrate each accomplishment.

5. *Bring in an "accountability" partner/coach.* It may be someone who is doing the plan with you so you can support each other, or it may be someone you trust to support you in a loving and powerful way. You can talk daily or every other day, but it should be consistent. THIS IS A VITAL PART OF YOUR POSSIBILITY PLAN.

6. ***Designate downtime***. Calendar in time to be still, read, pray, sleep and relax. This time must be a part of the process. Daily is best, and we all have busy schedules, but create at least two "significant" times just for you to rest and rejuvenate. DO NOT LET ANYONE OR ANYTHING GET IN THE WAY OF THIS TIME.

Speak this Possibility Affirmation/Declaration Daily:

Today, I am clear that my life is powerful and expansive. Every choice I make reinforces the unfolding of my dynamic destiny!

I AM CHOOSING ME

* * * * *

—*Pat Jacques*

It's not about becoming anything. It's about un-becoming almost everything!

—Sean Smith

I chose to participate in Cynthia James's Women's Mastermind program in order to move fully into my passion, my coaching practice. This work has been eye-and heart-opening, deep, fun, tearful, filled with laughter, and deeply supportive. Every so often I found myself chuckling. At first blush, some topics didn't feel like they fit. As my subconscious marinated these ideas and my body sat with the energy, I have had many startling "Ah-ha!" moments.

I spent a significant part of my life in fearful darkness, isolation, self-loathing and self-hatred. By nature, I was an energetic, joyful child, but I clearly got the message something "was not right" with me. When I asked Santa Claus for a "COWBOY outfit," I was disappointed to receive a "COWGIRL outfit." I experienced "body shaming" before we ever had that term. I was labeled as "husky" and then "fat", and hated that my nickname became "Fat Pat! Fat Pat!" I endured endless torture from children and adults alike. My teenage years and awakening to my sexuality deeply reinforced my shame.

In the Mastermind program, discussions and meditation about

"blocks" and "blind spots" initially did not elicit much from me. (We don't know what we don't know!) Days and weeks later, seemingly out of nowhere, I suddenly had epiphanies! During our small group work, while discussing healthy living challenges, I spoke these words for the umpteenth time: "My weight has always been my Achilles heel." Light bulb! Spirit had complied, and I manifested my belief. I made an intentional shift to saying, "Health and fitness come to me easily."

I honestly never gave much thought to "resistance." When asked to "invite resistance in, welcome her, and become friends with her," I sat quietly, not sure what to do. One meditation brought a message quickly. I needed to deepen my spiritual practice. (Which, of course, I'd heard from others, but nobody fights their own ideas! Right?) I consistently spoke evening gratitude prayers without fail, but I had become increasingly lax in my morning reading, journaling and meditation, and allowed myself to get sucked into the busyness of my high-tech life. I recommitted to my morning practice. Great! I was back on track! But there was more.

When I was introduced to Cynthia's "Daily Check-In" worksheet, I had yet another "Eureka!" moment. I'm well aware that acknowledging our efforts alone creates shift, but what if there is a way to "supercharge" that shift? Cynthia's simple method of choosing an area of focus, journaling about what is different, what is working and what isn't; recording the state of body, mind, and spirit; activating gratitude and setting an intention create a powerful mindset! Rather than simply recording what happened (past tense: can't do anything about it), I began a more systematic, mindful approach to each day.

Now I celebrate my efforts AND strategize next steps. This moves me from "motion" to "action." It also helped me with my biggest challenge, which was doing the work while managing my "busy" schedule. I became much clearer on how busy and full of motion I kept my day. Shifting to mindful intention created quiet, peace and deliberate action, which are rapidly and effortlessly moving me in the direction of my dreams.

My biggest revelation has been the realization that we all get **exactly** what we need! Women Creating Our Futures may have been a group project, but each participant had an incredibly personal experience. While my journey may have begun from a space of fear and isolation, I am now rooted in the knowing that I am always completely fully supported and loved. I stand in the awe and wonder of the unknown, allowing life to unfold. It is with absolute certainty that I say each and every one of us will have exactly the experience with all the wins, challenges, insights, and revelations that is in our highest and best interest.

My journey began as one of self-acceptance. It has grown to radical self-love! I still recall my abrupt, shocking realization that I came to this planet perfect just as I am. Whole! And complete! I have found my calling to inspire women to lead courageous, authentic and joyful lives. To see possibility, especially during challenges, I choose me by saying "yes" to my calling. I choose me by being compassionate and loving with myself, while holding myself to be accountable to be my highest and best. I choose me by getting out of my own way, by allowing the universe to flow through me, surround me, infuse me, and guide me.

CHAPTER THREE

PARENTING IS AN ART FORM

. . . . .

Children have never been very good at listening to their elders, but they have never failed to imitate them.

—James Baldwin

I don't remember who said this, but there really are places in the heart you don't even know exist until you love a child.

—Anne Lamott

When I entered my thirties, the urge to have children burst into my conscious awareness. I dreamed of having a little girl. I even named her Imani, which means faith in Swahili. The only thing missing from this amazing inner experience was a man to support this vision and build a life with me. Other women I knew were having children without a totally committed relationship, but that didn't sit well in my soul. I had no judgment about others; I just wanted a family and a man in my life who would be a great father to our children. Since I had grown up without a healthy, strong father figure, I was unwilling to try to raise a child alone. I had no problem connecting with men; I was attractive, smart and self-sufficient. However, since I had not done any personal development work, the men I attracted were in no way good husband or father material.

With each passing year, I grew more anxious about the clock ticking and the possibility of my never having children. Then, something miraculous happened: my manager introduced me to a man who saw me, was interested in connecting on a deep level and wanted a family. I was a little nervous because he was a celebrity and lived a lifestyle that was foreign to me. He was very upfront about the drug challenge he had struggled with and how committed he was to staying sober and building a life with someone. He had a biological son and a foster child living with him. He said he was ready to create a powerful marriage. We dove in, and our relationship became a private and public experience. After an incredible year, we got married, adopted the foster child and planned on having another child together. I was in my late thirties.

No one told me that blending a family would be so challenging. My stepson's mother hated that I was in the picture. That created non-supportive experiences and made it hard to bond with him. The son we adopted had come from living a challenging life in another state, and we were working hard to get him support in adjusting to a radical life change. My husband's career was booming, and I was juggling my acting career and home life.

I had never been a parent, and my husband had always relied on staff support with the children. I knew we needed to create a new foundation for parenting, but wasn't exactly clear about how to do it. Obviously, I couldn't look to my biological family for support. Those five years I was married brought me to my knees and pushed me into a life "parenting school" that forever changed me.

OLD PARADIGMS DON'T WORK

I had been on a spiritual path for some time and thought that I had really evolved. Oh, please...that was my first mistake. You know that thing you say about never going to be like your parents? Well, pretty quickly I realized that I was my mother, and I was even saying things she used to say to me that I hated. I became controlling, bossy, and wanted to dominate my children. I gave myself permission to do this because I told myself "it was for their own good." Yuck! That backfired big time. They rebelled, they argued, they defied me and they hid things from me. That made me feel more crazy. Finally, I went to a family therapist for help.

In our very first session the therapist said, "You are frustrated because the old paradigms of parenting no longer work. Children today want to be respected, honored and given the space to expand. They do want to be guided, but not bullied." I sat there with great sadness in my heart. I remembered wanting those very things in my childhood. How was it that I had become the thing I detested? Then, she said something profound: "You are an artist. Why don't you look at parenting as an art form?"

I went home and looked up the definition of art form:

1. The structure of an artistic work

2. A medium for artistic expression

3. Any medium regarded as having systematized rules, procedures or formulations

I began to contemplate how to turn my parenting into a creative experience. I knew my children needed a parent, not a friend. Many of the people in our community hung out with their kids, gave them no boundaries and were creating narcissistic, self-indulgent beings. I wanted my children to be healthy. So, I began to practice what I preached...and it was not easy.

I asked for family meetings so that we could communicate in a healthier way. I talked about my deep desire to change. I told them I needed structure in the house, and I wanted them to help me. I created a family contract of agreements that we all signed. They disliked that immensely, but it helped us all remember what we agreed to do. This process wasn't always clear, open or cohesive. We had to learn to trust each other. They had to see that I was really authentic in my desire to change.

I taught them how to wash clothes and we cooked together. Today, my youngest son is a chef. They had chores and got an allowance for getting them done on time. I know some people don't approve of this technique, but it gave them an entry into learning how to engage with and create a healthy relationship with money.

I asked them how they wanted to express themselves, and then I made it a priority to be at their sports events, find powerful art camps and invite their friends to our home. We even had morning "blessing times." Before school, we would sit in my bedroom and talk about how we wanted the day to go. Then, I would say a blessing. It was only a five-minute experience, but I always walked away feeling more bonded. If it looked like we were running late, they would say, "Aren't we going to do that blessing thing?"

One of the greatest gifts was our family "God Box." They didn't want to hear all of my spiritual conversation, but they were open to the fact that maybe a higher power could help us with life challenges. I suggested we create a God Box as a symbol of giving our problems to the Universe. They were boys and were clear they did not want a "girly" box. So they picked it. It was a Nike shoebox. We sealed it with tape and cut a small opening in the top. Then, throughout the year we would write, on a small piece of paper, anything that upset us, disappointed us or felt overwhelming. We would fold it and put our initials and the date on it. It was then dropped into the box and not opened until December

31. At that time, we read aloud to the family what was on the papers. We were often amazed how beautifully things had worked out. Then, we burned the papers and the box. We then created a new one for the next year. That tradition stayed with us through the divorce and through their teen years. I still have a God Box, and the kids will call and ask me to put something they struggle with into the box.

The marriage did not work out, and I did not have the opportunity to birth a child. However, I love being a mother. Parenting for me has been one of the greatest gifts in my life. After my divorce, I adopted the biological brother of the son I had adopted with my ex-husband. I believe that their bio-mom was the channel to bring my children to the planet. We have grown up together and I am so honored to be called "mom." I have learned to ask and not tell, to receive as well as give, to trust vulnerability and give thanks that the vision of being a parent looks different than I ever imagined. AND it is perfect for me.

YOUR CHILD NEEDS A PARENT, NOT A FRIEND

For my son's 11th birthday, I took him and his friends to Magic Mountain. It is an amusement park in the Los Angeles area known for its amazing roller coasters. I have to admit the visit was as much for me as it was for them. We were excited. We left our house early and got to the park as it opened. We stepped inside the gate and were met by one of the park characters. We were laughing and taking pictures as one of the little boys with us ran up to the character and hit it in the stomach. Those characters have "bodyguards," and the man stepped in immediately and threatened to eject us from the park. The little boy said, "My parents don't tell me what to do." I took him by the hand and told the man it would not happen again. Then I turned to the child and looked him in the eye.

"Your parents are not here," I said, "and what you just did is inappropriate." Then I looked at my son and said, "you all have two minutes to decide if you want to stay in this park. That means no more acting out!" I stepped aside to let the boys talk. My son came over and said, "We want to stay and no more hitting. I told him you were serious."

That moment was actually a time of great pride for me. My children know that I love them, and they also know that I am unwilling to allow behavior that is unkind. I believe children need love and boundaries. I lived in an affluent community back then, and many of the parents had no rules and relied on nannies to raise their children.

I was not interested in being my children's friend. I wanted to have a powerful relationship and give them the guidance they needed. Today, my children are loving, responsible and caring young men. They are also conscious parents.

We all want our children to like us. The question is, how far are you willing to go to be liked? I have worked with many teens who tell me that they want a parent who listens and understands them. They feel that it is nice to have someone you can hang out with, but it is better to be a child of someone who can support you in making healthy choices.

CHILDREN DO WHAT YOU DO, NOT WHAT YOU SAY

My children, like me, are pretty vocal. They have no problem sharing with me what they think about most subjects, especially when it comes to me being their mom. One day, I was reprimanding my youngest son. He looked at me and said, "Why should I listen? You do the same thing." My ego definitely had leaped into space. I got triggered, and an ugly disagreement unfolded. When I got to my room and became quiet, I had an epiphany: I never listened to what *my* mother said. I watched what she did. In fact, many of the things I decided **not to do** came as a result of wanting to be a different parent than my mother on some levels.

We are all products of our home life and conditioning. We cannot expect our children to do better than what we model. I remember that a girlfriend of mine from high school became pregnant, and her mother was furious. That fact amazed me, since her mother had a constant parade of men through their home from the time my friend was a very young child.

Here is a reality check: if you keep a messy house, it probably won't go well to ask your children to keep their rooms clean. If you tell "little white lies," you cannot reprimand your children for lying. If you drink and smoke dope a lot, it might be challenging to ask your children to not drink or do drugs. They will do what you do, not what you tell them to do.

From my perspective, parenting has to be about living what we say we believe. It is about walking our talk and inviting our children to do the same. It has to be about teaching our children to be the best they can be and bringing their unique light to this world.

PARENTING EXERCISES

• • • • •

I am not a parenting expert, but here are some tools I learned that might support you in creating healthier experiences with your children.

MODEL WHO YOU WANT THEM TO BE

» When you make a mistake, take responsibility and apologize. There is no such thing as a "flawless" parent.

» Share your decision-making processes. Kids need to know they have choice and how decisions can affect lives and relationships.

» Take care of yourself. They learn self-care from you. Being still is a great way to model the power of silence.

LEARN TO LISTEN

» Create time to listen to them without trying to fix. They will begin to open up and share more deeply.

» Be interested and curious about what lights them up.

» Ask them what they need when they share a hurtful or painful experience.

» Even the music they like can teach powerful lessons.

TELL THE TRUTH

» Trust is achieved through honest interaction.

» Your vulnerability teaches them it is okay to feel and express.

» Share your challenges: they need to learn that life isn't always easy.

TEACH THEM HOW TO SERVE

» Invite them to join you in service to the community. (Church or spiritual communities are great resources.)

» Have them shop for, wrap and deliver gifts for under-privileged kids. (My children did this for several years.)

» Invite them to support elderly people in the community. (Take out trash, shovel sidewalks, mow the lawn.)

INVITE THEM TO EXPLORE THEIR SPIRITUAL NATURE

» Talk about different religions.

» If they want to visit churches, synagogues or temples, say yes.

» Show them how to connect with the spirit of nature.

» Share ways to center and meditate to lessen their stress. There are great meditation tapes and books for kids.

GIVE CONSISTENT "LOVE TAPS"

» Send a text telling them how amazing they are.

» Call when you know they are busy and leave a message telling them you love them.

» Post a picture of you with them on social media.

» Send an email reminding them how grateful you are that they are in your life.

BEFRIENDING TIME

. . . . .

—Kay M. Adams

It was 6:02 a.m. on a Friday, and I was sitting alone in the early morning light, enjoying a few moments of stolen silence while my family slept. I was nursing my first cup of coffee and trying to wash the cobwebs from my brain when my precious 5-year-old son Eli came sleepily walking into the kitchen in his well-worn robot pajamas with the words "I am programmed for hugs" on the front of them. His favorite stuffed animal, "Green Bean," was in one arm and a cozy blanket was trailing after him in the other. He crawled onto my lap in the dining room chair and snuggled against my body with his long legs dangling over the side of the chair. He sat quietly for a few luxurious minutes, nestled on my chest, before he began to speak. He softly whispered, "Mama, can you please read me a few chapters in my new book before you go to work today? Oh, please?!"

I looked up at the clock on the kitchen wall that read 6:10 a.m., and was instantly torn between my allegiances and the competing demands for my time and attention. There was absolutely *nothing* I would rather have done in that moment than snuggle and read to my beloved boy—reveling in our "moment of bliss" together. But I still had breakfast to eat, lunches to pack, a shower to take, and dishes to do before I left for work by 7:00. This was not a day where I had any wiggle room to spare in my schedule. My patients were waiting for me, and I couldn't be late. I wrestled with the concept of time in my mind and cursed the scarcity of it in that instant. I had wasted so much of it in my youth when it appeared to be an endless commodity, and now, in moments like these, I longed for every second of it back. So, as much as it pained me to do so, I had to tell Eli that I couldn't read those stories that morning because I still had many jobs to do before leaving for work, and I had to get started. Eli looked up at me with those beautiful blue eyes, filled with tears and disappointment, and mumbled, "Okay, Mama. Maybe you can read them to me tonight when you get home." With a grieving heart, I headed for the shower, but I could never wash the image of Eli's sad face from my consciousness—no matter how hard I tried.

Unfortunately, that day is similar to most in my life since becoming a parent at the age of 48. Ever since Eli's birth, I have been trying to juggle the myriad of obligations to my son, my spouse, my employer, and myself simultaneously, without dropping any of the spinning plates above my head in the process. Some days I manage fairly well, and other days I fail completely and the plates come crashing down to the floor in broken shards all around me.

I catch myself saying "I don't have time" as an instantaneous response to my life. In fact, it's become an ingrained habit, an unintentional mantra and message that The Universe hears loud and clear—and one that no longer serves my highest good. And so I am working on changing my relationship with time as I work towards creating a life of my dreams. I am now clear that time is a finite resource and, because of that, I need to become a better steward of it. I want to dedicate my time towards sharing my gifts with the world, spending quality time with my family and friends, following my heart-felt passions, and shining my brightest light for all to see.

As the journey unfolds, the obvious challenge will be balancing my personal and professional commitments. I have come to realize the precarious balance in which I live, and it is unsettling at best. When I devote time to one area of my life, it takes away from another. When I pursue one dream, another may die on the vine. When I constantly give myself away to others, I often don't have anything left for myself. That is simply no longer acceptable to me.

I now understand that I have the power within myself to choose differently with my time than I did in my youth. I am older now and much wiser, and every year I grow closer to the end of my life than to its beginning. I can't change my past, but I can embrace and plan for a future where my regrets are few and my joys are many—one step at a time. Thankfully, I now possess the seasoned awareness necessary to choose me first at this spiritual crossroad in my life, and I am powerfully choosing to work towards manifesting a life lived on my terms, and aligned with my core values, before any more precious time runs out. And that is exactly what I plan to do.

YOUR WORK LIFE

This section focuses on the many facets of being successful at work. The intention is to support you whether you are an entrepreneur, working for someone else or building your dream life. Use this information to create a toolbox of ways to take your work life to the next level.

CHAPTER FOUR

CREATING LIFE ON YOUR TERMS

· · · · ·

You cannot control what happens to you, but you can control your attitude toward what happens to you, and in that, you will be mastering change rather than allowing it to master you.

—Brian Tracy

"I am powerless to change my destiny!" That was the thought that was coursing through my mind as I sat in a room of executives who were panicked that they were going to lose their biggest client. Everyone was desperate to find the perfect presentation to keep the client engaged. I, on the other hand, was focused on the fact that I was in the wrong place, and felt that I had no way out. I felt like I needed this job to take care of my family and myself. I needed the money to stay afloat. I could have cared less about the drama in the room except that I knew if they didn't keep this account, jobs—including mine—would be in jeopardy.

In the blink of an eye, my mind left the space and moved into some kind of altered reality. I could see myself being happy and successful. I could see myself speaking to hundreds of people and signing books.

I could see myself teaching to groups all around the world. As my attention returned to the space, I wanted to cry. My mind screamed, "You better get hold of yourself!" I looked down at the paper in front of me and began to doodle so that no one would see how distraught I was. There was no way that this dream was going to be a reality. I was locked inside a prison of my own making.

Amelia Earhart once said, "The most difficult thing is the decision to act, the rest is merely tenacity. The fears are paper tigers. You can do anything you decide to do. You can act to change and control your life, and the procedure, the process is its own reward."

So, there I was, sitting at that table. I took a breath and a thought came flying in: "Re-invent yourself. You have always done that." It was true. I had re-created myself hundreds of times. Why was this any different? I looked around the room once more. No one looked happy. It was then that I made a decision. I told myself, "I am the captain of my life-ship and I can take control of how I live, in this very moment." I didn't have to know how, I didn't have to know when; I just had to take action. I had to make a move, or be stuck here a year from now feeling just as miserable.

Let me say here that I come from a long line of women who were masterful at "controlling" space and others. I think some people would even say they were master manipulators. I knew that I wanted to be in control of myself, but I didn't want to live like the women in my familial line. Life was calling me, and I wanted to change the trajectory of my unfolding destiny without playing the game of controlling others to get what I want.

There is a big difference in taking control and being controlling. The definition of control is "the power to influence or direct people's behavior or the course of events."

It was clear that I had to find a way to change the course of events in my life. I was currently operating out of fear, desperation and doubt.

I was never going to live the life of my dreams looking at life through this lens. I did not have to change the organization I worked for or their perspective on success. I did not have to stay in a space of feeling constricted. I didn't need to have dominion over anything or anyone but myself. However, it was clear that if I stayed in this place, I would continue to re-create my current reality. It was in that moment that I caught the spark of the notion that I - and only I - could change my life.

When the meeting completed, I got up from the seat, walked to my desk and took out a pad. I wrote, "In one year I will be doing what I love!" That moment was pivotal for me.

I would love to tell you that the next year was easy and I just flowed into my greater yet-to-be. Unfortunately, it was filled with those paper tiger fears and lots of false starts. In retrospect, I can see that every step - every action, every wrong move and every decision - was a distinct part of my evolution. The only way to get to another place is to start and put one foot in front of the other.

YOU ARE THE ONLY ONE IN CONTROL OF YOUR LIFE

As a child, I was always looking for approval. I wanted someone, anyone, to validate that I was important, smart, supported and loved. My family was too dysfunctional to give it to me. My friends were from the same or worse familial structures and most of my teachers were clueless; that is, except Mr. Benson and Ms. Milke. For some reason, both of these teachers saw me. They understood that I was intelligent and had gifts. Instead of angry reprimands or ignoring my outbursts, each of these teachers invited me to explore my creativity and brilliance.

I remember sitting at a desk feeling upset that I was stuck on a math problem. Math was one of my worst subjects. Mr. Benson leaned over next to me. He said, "Do you have any idea how powerful you are? I know you are here to do great things. How about you pause for a moment and then go back to the problem in front of you. I know you can do this." He didn't take the power away from me or say, "Let me show you how." I did what he said and I solved the problem. I was so proud of myself.

He had only asked me to stop and find the solution within me. It wasn't until I was a grown up that I finally remembered that very simple act of empowerment. Once I did, I constantly went back to that moment in my mind to get back on track.

The important lesson that took me a long time to learn was that there is no one outside of you who can tell you what is best for you. Teachers and mentors can guide you. Friends and family can support and give suggestions, but you are the only one that can "know" 100% what is right for you. Every time you give yourself and your power to someone else, you deny the greatness that exists at your core. You pull your incredible "spark of the divine" out of the equation.

There is no one who can do what you came to do the way only you can do it. There is no other person on the planet who can deliver your gifts. Could it be as simple as "pausing" and learning to listen to that still, small voice within you that is connected to a powerful source? Yes, it is; the caveat is that the pause might take longer than you want. It might take days or months to get still and clear enough to connect to the beautiful intuitive being that you are and have always been. The key is to practice "inner listening."

Most of us have not been trained to listen to the quiet voice of intuition. We have been told to "think about it," "find the solution in our minds," or "come up with a strategy to get you where you want to go." All of those things are nice, but they will keep you spinning in a web of monkey-mind scenarios.

BALANCE IS AN INSIDE JOB

I don't do anything halfway. Once I decide, I am all in. That is the good and "interesting" news.

The good news is that I will work hard. I will do enormous research.

I will create amazing products and be in service to people and projects in extraordinary ways.

The interesting news is that I will have forgotten to eat, rest, work out and simply take care of myself.

Needless to say, the "interesting" part does not support my health and well-being. It keeps me on an adrenaline high and running on empty a lot.

From my perspective, balance is really about harmony. It is about a harmonic convergence of doing and being. It is about consciously deciding that no life is actually fulfilled if you are working all of the time. It is also not fulfilled by doing so much for others that you cannot find any room for self-nurturing.

From my perspective, there are three areas to consider.

» **Stillness** – You must have time daily to just unplug. That might mean meditation, sitting alone, journaling thoughts and desires, taking a nap or just sitting down with nothing to do. There is a reason that monks ensconced in deep daily practices of stillness have healthier minds and brain activity. I spend 45 minutes a day in meditation, journaling and prayer. I start each day with this practice to anchor stillness in my being.

» **Journaling** – James W. Pennebaker, a professor in Austin, Texas, did extensive research on writing to heal. His work uncovered the power of writing to up-level the immune system and support overall health. Many of us don't like to write but, according to his research, writing just five minutes a day could change your life. Stream of consciousness journaling is writing with no particular focus. It is about putting your random thoughts on paper. Those thoughts could be about joy, creativity, anger, upset or deep desires. Whatever comes out is there to support your health and well-being. Julia Cameron created The Artist's Way process. She suggests writing three "morning pages" every day that let the subconscious bring form to hidden treasures. You can do it your way, but what is imperative is that you find time to pause, get quiet and get your thoughts out on paper.

» **Conscious Connections** – Being with people who feed your soul is essential. Some of those people might be connected to business, and some might not be. What is important is that these are people who do not require you to be in any form of "performance" mode. They recognize you and just want to be in your company. It doesn't matter if you share deep desires or just stand together in the silence. Selecting these people will take some time because most of our family, friends and colleagues want something from us. Conscious connections nurture the quietude within us, and invite us to expand beyond our limited thinking. I have a couple of friends who do this for me, and the moment we connect, I just exhale and relax.

THE TIME IS NOW!

You have a brilliant mind. It is designed to think and create. It is also designed to regurgitate what you feed it. Most of us have been conditioned to look for the worst and create entire "mind movies" that are fueled by limited thinking.

The only time you have is now. This is the moment. Whatever you choose right now will be a creative mechanism to manifest in the world you live in. It will out-picture in relationships, work environments, collaborations and health. So, it seems to me that it is important to get clear about the choices that you are making right now.

When I was dating the man who is now my ex-husband, I knew there was a possibility of great challenge if we married. He was charming, handsome, wealthy and celebrated in his field. He also had a long track record of drug abuse and rehab experiences. After a brief separation during which I supported him in getting clean, we decided to marry. I remember that on the day before the wedding, I asked myself if this was the right choice. He hadn't been sober very long. I had a long history of failed relationships. Had I done enough work? Was our love strong enough to keep us anchored? Those thoughts were quickly brushed aside as the excitement of the moment rushed in. My family was excited. We were in a foreign country and the energy of the fantastic life we were creating blocked any sense of reason or intuition.

As I look back now, I can see that the "little" thought was a gentle universal nudge. It was telling me that this choice had consequences that were far-reaching. I do not regret the choice; it helped me become the person that I am today. However, I am clear that the pain that ensued could have been avoided if I had just listened to the still, small voice and paused.

I believe that every situation, experience and choice is part of the path of discovery that we all must travel to stimulate our true potential. I also believe that being awake in each moment allows us to choose experiences that can accelerate thriving and extraordinary living.

You do not have to wait to wake up. You do not have to have all your ducks in a row before you take a leap into the unknown. However, it is advisable to make sure you peruse your motives, intentions and desired outcomes. If you keep doing what you have done before, you **will** create the same result.

LIFE CREATION EXERCISES

· · · · ·

It is important to get clear on the kind of questions you ask yourself. Before making any changes, ask yourself these questions and journal your responses.

» Do the people around me lift me up and support my dreams?

» Am I doing something daily to create the life I want to live?

» Do I have goals and a vision that ignite the passion within me?

» Do I have reminders in my home or office (affirmations or a vision board) that support my big life?

» Have I created a timeline for completing my projects?

HERE IS A WAY TO PUT YOUR DREAM INTO ACTION:

1. Write down what ignites you and brings you joy.

2. Write down what you would be doing if there were nothing in the way.

3. Write down how living in your passion could be of service.

Now, considering these three things, create an intention statement no longer than 3-4 lines. Write it down, post it where you can see it, and say it out loud three times a day without fail. You do not have to know how it will come about; just activate the possibility and be open to trusting that it is possible for you to answer your call and be fully supported. *(Example: I am here to thrive and deliver my gifts in powerful ways. I am fully supported and I soar!)*

MEDITATION

• • • • •

Sit back and relax. Gently close your eyes and begin to breathe. Allow yourself to activate your imagination. See yourself living a life of passion. See yourself joyous. See yourself financially free. See yourself in service by sharing your gifts. How does it feel? Allow that feeling to expand within you. Now let that feeling fill the room. Let it move out of the space you occupy and fill the city in which you live. Let it move across the country, across the ocean until that energy is shining brightly around the world. Breathe that in and enjoy the feeling. Now, return to your current space with that expanded feeling fully ignited. If in the next few days doubt tries to crop up and get in the way, bring this feeling back into your body. Anything is possible and your dream would not be there if there were not a way to fulfill it. Continue to stay with that vision for a minimum of ten minutes. Then, re-connect to the breath and slowly bring your attention back to the room in which you sit.

Feel free to journal what you saw and felt. It will anchor the experience.

A MATTER OF THE HEART

* * * * *

—Renee Featherstone

It was hard to control my excitement when my cousins told me they got tape recorders for Christmas. I blurted out, "I have a tape recorder, too!"

"No, you don't," their mom said.

"Yes, I do," I protested. "I got it for Christmas."

"Well, you don't have it anymore because your dad pawned it."

"No, he didn't, because I saw it in my closet this morning."

"Well, it must be an empty box because your father brought it in this week," she said.

She thought she knew everything just because her husband owned the pawn shop.

"I'm going home right now to get it. I'll show you."

It took two minutes to run across the street and grab the tape recorder out of my closet. Only it wasn't a tape recorder at all. It was a picture of the tape recorder I got for Christmas on the empty box. It felt like someone had knocked the wind out of me. To this day, I don't know why this was so hard to take - maybe because everyone knew what happened except me.

My father was/is a gambler, so I was accustomed to things "disappearing," like when my mother and I spent months saving and pasting Blue Chip stamps so I could get a new bicycle from their catalog and the stamps disappeared. I was disappointed, but not surprised. By then, I was well seasoned. I had experienced moving frequently, always in the middle of the school year, and sometimes at night. "Lending" my dad money I received as gifts and never getting it back. Having our utilities disconnected on occasion felt normal.

I had learned to expect disappointment. There were the promises of a fun day at Disneyland or Knotts Berry Farm, which always seemed to end with my mom saying, "Honey, I'm too tired. Maybe next week." Or, "we don't have enough money, let's see after payday." At that time, I was unaware of the burdens my mother carried because my father worked very hard at not working, and gambling away the money she worked hard for. She found it challenging to pay the bills and put food on our table, especially when she added a weekly payment to the hit man so her three children could have a father. There were times she would not eat unless there was food left after her kids had eaten.

Although my dad appeared to have an equal affinity for women and playing horses, it was finally his female indiscretions that caused my mom to throw in the towel. To this day, I'm not sure which had the deepest effect on me, but one of the most memorable experiences was a Saturday morning after my parents separated. My mother's eyes had become permanently red and swollen, and her clothes hung on her. The air in our apartment was thick with pain. There was no light to cut through it.

When there was a knock on the door, it was my job as the oldest to answer it. The woman at the door said, "I'm looking for Roger. He stole all my furniture." I remember running to my mom's room to tell her. I don't have a vivid recollection of her response, but it was in that instant that I decided I never wanted to feel the kind of pain that my mom was feeling. I committed in that moment to protect my heart in every way possible.

I enjoyed dating in college, but always knew how to end a relationship as soon as I saw any sign of imperfection. If you're thinking imperfection exists in every relationship, you're right; which is why I was always the one to end the relationship. I left men baffled and often hurt. To make things easier, I began to tell them upfront that I only did relationships for two weeks. My reasoning was that everyone is always on his or her best behavior in the first two weeks. They started being themselves and the fantasy of a fun and exciting union was over, and so was I.

It took two marriages and lots of therapy to see that I had never been willing to open my heart. The first man I finally opened my heart to as a woman helped me to realize my worst fear. He represented my father in that, unbeknownst to me, he was married. My heart was broken, but I decided that, even though it was painful, the loving part was so good that I was willing to leave my heart open to experience such ecstasy.

Ecstasy was what I experienced for nine years with my third husband. The tenth year brought an unspeakable betrayal—my personal 9-11. It took about a year to climb from under the rubble and debris. With the help of a therapist, I rebounded with a very healthy mind and spirit. A physical exam indicated I had good blood pressure, great cholesterol and perfect BMI. I was in great shape and I felt good.

It was approximately a month or so later that I found myself in the ER, having had a heart attack. Despite having good exam results and no family history, I had a heart attack with a 90% blockage in an artery. The doctors said it was "the luck of the draw." They said I was just unlucky. I began to wonder, if I had a 90% blockage in my physical heart, what percentage of blockage did I have in my emotional heart?

So here I am five years later, truly healthy in mind, body and spirit because I decided to choose me this time in a healthy way. I now choose me by practicing daily rituals of meditation, physical movement and gratitude journaling. I choose to love myself unconditionally. I choose to forgive myself. I choose to consciously keep my heart open, no matter how scary it is. I choose to live!

CHAPTER FIVE

Powerful Parallel-Preneurship

• • • • •

*Strategic planning for your business may mean hiring
new people, investing in technology & figuring out how
to put those resources to use.*

—Susie Carder

I have never worked one job at a time in my life. I was always working at one job for money and one for "doing what I love" on the side. In high school, I worked as a carhop (I know I am dating myself) while I was a singing in a local band. It felt as though my life depended upon doing something that I was passionate about to stay sane and connected to my life goals. Over time, I continued this pattern with the intention of living the life of my dreams. Here are some of the jobs that funded those dreams:

» Data entry clerk to pay my way through college

» Airline hostess while studying to sing

» Media sales rep while going to school for Communications

» Urban development assistant while trying to break into television

» Dancer in a Las Vegas show while studying to be an actress

» Hostess at Denny's to give me time to audition for acting and singing parts

» Receptionist while studying acting with renowned coach Stella Adler

» Executive assistant while getting a degree in spiritual psychology, ministerial training, building my counseling practice, writing my first book and recording two CD's

It is not that I wasn't operating well in the jobs. I had some amazing experiences. I learned a lot and gained skills that are utilized as part of my business today. In many cases, I was in great service and supported myriads of people. The challenge was that I was slowly and efficiently burning myself out. At one point, my doctor told me that my adrenals were compromised and strongly suggested I quit my job. Instead, I took a sabbatical to try and "figure out" how I could find a way to manage the life I had created.

It never dawned on me at the time that there was a name for my madness. A few years ago, I was sitting in a Lisa Nichols/Motivating The Masses class, and I heard the term "parallel-preneur." I thought, oh, that's me. The next thought, which was actually a question, is what began a breakthrough: "Why do you always have to do something that you are not totally passionate about to make money?" That question stopped me in my tracks. I felt nauseated and a flood of shame entered the space. Here I was teaching people to stand in their power, bring their dreams to life, find their voice and create sustainable income doing what they loved, all the while not doing it myself. Sadness flooded my entire being and I felt like a fraud.

A mind battle began. One side reminded me of all my accomplishments and the difference I had made in the lives of people around the globe. The other side scolded me for being so afraid to step out and leap fully into my destiny. It reminded me that I had built "kingdoms" for many people and organizations. When was it my turn?

Those inner dialogues kept me awake at night. The internal conflict was intense, and it became clear that I was being called to take action. I had to make a different choice. I had to move away from the fear inside of me and dare to move in the direction of my dreams. I was a parallel-preneur at this moment, but I didn't have to stay one.

I got very intentional, and created a plan to move into being a full-time entrepreneur. Let me say here, there were moments of doubt in my abilities, fear of the unknown and deep concern about my financial stability as I moved forward. I was letting go of a "sure thing" and, if I failed, I had no backup. My husband reminded me that I had always been successful, and encouraged me to trust that I would be supported. His voice inside my head often pulled me back off the edge of the cliff of uncertainty.

Here are the three principles that I used to move to where I am today:

LOVING WHAT YOU DO TAKES CLARITY AND FOCUS

When someone would ask me what I did for a living, I gave this long-winded explanation. I would see a blank look in their eyes and I knew I had lost them. I was absolutely opposed to using an "elevator speech" because, personally, I could feel the inauthenticity whenever anyone gave me a canned explanation of his or her business. I wanted to be sincere and enthusiastic about what I did. I wanted people to get excited with me and want to know more. I decided to write down what I love about what I do in the world. What came forward were a series of statements that I knew inspired me.

» I love **reminding** people that they are here to live **extraordinary** lives.

» I love **inspiring** people to awaken to their purpose and power... but women are my primary followers.

» I love **teaching** and **speaking** to seekers about health and transformation.

» I love teaching how to navigate the stormy waters of **emotional upheaval.**

» I love sharing **practical tools** for everyday living in mind, body and spirit.

» I love infusing **creativity and movement** into the delivery of my message.

» I love **traveling** and **guiding** people to magical places on the planet.

What I do: inspire, teach, speak, travel and guide.

Who I do it for: seekers, especially women, ready to awaken to their purpose, health and transformation.

How I do it: teaching people to live powerful lives in mind, body and spirit by navigating emotional challenges and utilizing practical tools for extraordinary health and well-being. Bringing creativity and movement into the ways I deliver my message.

Mission: To inspire seekers to live extraordinary, healthy and purposeful lives in mind, body and spirit

This mission became the foundation for the delivery system of my work. Now it was time to move into action. We all have separate dreams, but there are some things that support all "dream builders."

» Get clear about your vision.

» Create a timeline.

» Be honest about your current reality.

» Identify the resources you need to meet your timeline.

» Get an accountability coach or partner.

» Do something daily to manifest your dreams.

Do what you MUST to create the life you love

Once I got clear about the mission, I knew the next step was creating more of what I loved to do. That meant I had to come up with a plan to create space and time to live the life of my dreams. This was not going to be so easy: my life was jam-packed.

First, I needed a deadline. I don't know about you, but without one, I just wander and time passes me by. So, I pulled out my calendar and budget sheets. I knew enough not to make any rash moves. I am not a linear person by nature, but I understood that, in this instance, clarity was necessary and essential. I made a list of questions in areas I needed focus. Here is the list:

» How much money do I need to save to take care of myself once I leave the security of my job?

» How much do I need to invest to learn what I don't know about being an entrepreneur? (I was crystal clear that every entrepreneur invests and re-invests in their business. I needed capital to do that.)

» What was it going to cost me to market my business to another level?

» What kind of team do I need to support me and what can I afford to spend to pay them?

» How many clients and or engagements do I need each quarter to fiscally support my business and me in the next year?

The answer to these questions took time and planning. I had to sit down with my accountant and get real about my current reality. I then invited someone I respected in marketing to support me in creating a plan that I could follow to increase my visibility and attract clients. Now, I was ready to get a different kind of support to take me to the next level.

POWERFUL MENTORS ACCELERATE THE PROCESS

I have worked for and supported many communities and organizations. There was a deep desire to grow inside these organizations, and yet old paradigms, beliefs or timing thwarted their ability to move to the next level of success. I knew some of those fears lived in me and an already successful mentor would support me greatly. I needed to find someone doing what I do, and doing it at a higher level.

My husband is a member of a transformational leadership organization, and all of the members are successful entrepreneurs, authors, teachers and speakers. I was at one of their meetings and Lisa Nichols was standing near me. Lisa Nichols is CEO of Motivating the Masses, a teacher in the movie *The Secret,* a bestselling author and world-renowned speaker. Her business created the term, "Parallel-Preneurship." All of a sudden, it was as if something was propelling me towards her. I found myself saying, "I would like for you to mentor me."

She smiled and said, "Mentoring takes time, and I don't have a lot of it in this moment. However, I will **gift** you a weekend at my Global Leadership Program in San Diego next month. You just need to get there and see if there is support for you." I was stunned at her generosity. The very next thought was, "I have too much on *my* calendar." Those of us who are parallel-preneurs ALWAYS have too much on our plates. So, in that moment, I decided - I was being offered a chance to grow and become someone who does what I want to do in the world..."Clear the Calendar!" That is exactly what I did. I cancelled all of my appointments, bought a ticket and booked a hotel room. Those actions proved to be one of the greatest gifts of my life.

Lisa's team are all experts in the areas in which I needed to expand. I was excited and a little intimidated. There was so much I didn't know. I sat there and remembered that I am a quick learner and, once I have learned something, I am great at focus and implementation. That was the moment of a great leap of faith. I invested in a year-long program to be mentored by Lisa and her team. The program was not easy. I was being asked to look at my limiting beliefs. I was being asked to stretch in the ways I created my business and how I called in clients and handled my fiscal responsibilities. I had no idea how much I didn't know AND I was 100% committed to learning and becoming a powerful and independent entrepreneur.

The insight I also gained was that I was already doing a lot that was right. I had amazing "content." I had built a wonderful platform of followers who felt served by my message and gifts. Many of my current clients were happy and feeling empowered. My job was to expand each area.

In summary, I was clueless in some areas and knew I had to be humble and ask for help. There were moments of feeling complete vulnerability and confusion. However, I was determined. I had invested this money, and I was going to dive in full force. **Many people take a leap and forget that the commitment to follow through feeds the success.** If I failed, it would not be because I did not try full out. I needed to understand how to bring my most authentic self to the world, engage more of my followers and be more in service to their needs. I wanted to make more money, but expansion meant delivering more to everyone I touched. It was not easy, and there were times I was frustrated and annoyed with myself. I just kept putting one foot in front of the other.

In one year, my client base grew; I opened an office and began to build an expanded speaking business. I exceeded my goals and brought in enough money to pay for my investment, my bills and myself.

Many leaders tell us to "model" those who are doing what we desire to do. My question to you is, "What are you doing to get mentored into greatness?" There is someone in this world who can serve and support you in moving to the next level. You do not have to work as a parallel-preneur unless you truly want to do that. I believe that the only thing that is required in this moment is to seek out the support you need to grow.

CLARITY EXERCISES

• • • • •

ASK POWERFUL QUESTIONS

These are the questions I used. Use them as a starting point and then add others that make sense for your business. Do not rush through these. The answers will fuel your decisions moving forward.

» Why do I want to do this work or create this vision?

» What is the problem my gift/work is solving?

» Who are the ideal people waiting for my product or service?

» Am I committed to doing what it takes to bring this dream to life?

» What kind of support do I need to make this happen?

ACTIVELY SEEK OUT A MENTOR

When you look for a mentor/coach, it is important that you focus on someone who is doing what you want to do in the world. Do some research to support your decision on who to select as your coach. Make sure that they are accessible to you and can communicate in a style that feels supportive.

This might be a virtual experience. Many successful people have online programs, teleseminars and webinars to support people in growing. You really want to be sure that the programs offered will support your learning style. Many creatives find it hard to work online all of the time. If you are one of those people, it would be best to find a program/coach that offers some personal interaction.

I work with people in person via Skype, workshops and through online programs. This gives people the opportunity to choose what works best for them. I also create custom plans for people who want to work in an accelerated way.

You also want to look at what they charge. Do they have payment plans? What are the outcomes they are telling you will be delivered? You want to be clear before you commit. Lisa's programs were perfect for me because they were a combination of in-person meetings, teleconferences and one-on-one phone coaching.

Here are some questions to help you identify mentors:

- » Are they doing what I want to do and doing it successfully?
- » What are they doing that attracts me to them?
- » What things do I want to learn from them?
- » What strengths do I have that they can help me amplify?
- » What weaknesses do I have that they can assist me in shifting?
- » Am I willing to be accountable?
- » Am I willing to listen and act with focus and consistency?
- » Am I willing to invest in a way that will stretch me?
- » Am I ready to move forward no matter what others think about my expansion?

LIVE YOUR PASSION

• • • • •

—Cheryl Burget

It was 6:15 a.m. on June 23, 2005.

As the phone rang, I looked at the caller ID. It read: "Denver Children's Hospital."

My heart began to beat faster and I thought to myself, *This isn't going to be good news.*

"Hello," I answered in an anxious voice.

"Hi, Cheryl, it's Bridget. I hope I didn't disturb you, but I need your help." As my friend's voice quivered, she explained how her seven-year-old son, Blake, had just been diagnosed with cancer. She began to describe how the doctor discovered a large tumor the size of a grapefruit in his chest.

As I stood shocked, trying to comprehend what I was hearing, I couldn't hold back the tears. Trying to steady myself, I said, "Oh, Bridget, I am sorry. How can I help? I will do anything you need, just let me know."

Feeling worried, helpless and bewildered, I was still trying to process what I had just heard. She had seen me through so many ups and downs during the last ten years of our friendship that I thought I never would have the chance to repay her. Sadly, now I could.

You see, my friend Bridget was the one I affectionately called "my voice of reason." She was my wise, trusted confidante; the one I always went to for advice. She seemed to be living the all-American life: a well-paying corporate job, a beautiful home, two lovely children and a supportive partner. It was in that moment that I realized anything can happen without notice, no preparation...I was shocked into a new life reality.

After 13 months of chemotherapy, radiation and a stem cell transplant, the cancer was too strong for his little body. As I spoke to Bridget the day before he passed, she said with heartbreaking anguish, "I am not ready to say goodbye." And then I heard the words, "You don't have to say goodbye, just say 'I'll see you later.'" I repeated the words to her in hopes of offering something softer than the finality of goodbye for the heart-wrenching moments that were coming too quickly. On July 19, 2006, Blake lost his battle with lymphoblastic lymphoma and leukemia.

As I painfully watched my grieving friend and her family try to cope with losing Blake, I began a relentless quest to understand why. It was during this time that I had a new awareness: life can change in an instant. To honor Blake, I would live my life more consciously, follow my heart and intuition, and seek divine meaning.

From the time I was very young, I remember believing I would grow up, go to college and end up in a corporate job with an impressive title and a corner office, in that order. While I spent 17 successful years in the financial services industry, I had accomplished what I once believed was "success," and more than I believed I could achieve, yet something was missing. I remember leaving my office one day, wondering if I would ever experience happiness and fulfillment in my job again. That year was 2006.

I had been questioning my future during the time Blake was sick but, when he passed that next year, I accelerated my search for more meaning and purpose. I began to seriously question: "what was my true purpose on this planet?"

I wondered, "what could I do that would make a difference and also get that joy and happiness back?" Just as the universe always answers with a solution, for me it was to attend a program with the authors of *The Passion Test*. The authors described how our passions are clues to our purpose. During the weekend workshop, I discovered that one of my passions was to inspire others to find their own greatness, and empower them to live it. Something else I learned from that weekend was that "I didn't have to know the how." *Great*, I thought, because I didn't have any idea *how* I was going to do this while working full time with a ten-state territory, selling investment strategies to brokers and financial planners.

Then I realized that what I loved about working with my clients was having an ability to help them solve their problems by providing solutions I believed in. So, with the instability of the financial markets and no end in sight, I could no longer stand to see my clients lose millions of dollars for which I could not control.

I had been patiently waiting for a clear strategy to come to me on how to make the leap into a new career and find the financial resources to do so. Step-by-step, the "how" began to unfold.

The first opportunity came when I received an early morning call from one of the authors of *The Passion Test*, inviting me to become a Master Trainer for their certified facilitator program. I hardly waited for her to finish the invitation before I said, "Yes."

So, I began the journey to become the first Master Trainer for *The Passion Test*, which continued for the next eight years. In the beginning, I had known that the opportunity alone would not offer me enough income, so I waited for the next "how."

Over the next few months, it slowly became clear how I could transition into a way to live my purpose more fully. In the moments I felt fear rising within me during this transition, I would repeat what has become my own personal mantra, "Choose faith over fear." And so, on October 1, 2007, I resigned from my corporate life and began stepping into my true passion and purpose.

What I have learned is that each of us has a unique purpose and timeframe for leaving our imprint. That young boy's courage, strength and wisdom during his eight-year journey through cancer continued to encourage me as I followed my own journey, living my passion and purpose. Indeed, over a very short time, Blake had left a lifetime of lessons which continue to impact many people, like myself, who were touched by his life.

CHAPTER SIX

EXPANDING VISIBILITY

. . . . .

Make visible what, without you, might perhaps never have been seen.

—Robert Bresson

Wherever you are, that is your platform, your stage, your circle of influence. That is your talk show and that is where your power lies. In every way, in every day, you are showing people exactly who you are. You're letting your life speak for you. And when you do that, you will receive in direct proportion to how you give in whatever platform you have.

— Oprah Winfrey

Resistance! Resistance! Resistance! That is the only way to describe how I have dealt with becoming more visible in the world. You would not know that if you looked at the path of my life. There has never been any place, organization or experience where I did not ascend to being in leadership or a primary state of visibility.

Clearly, my destiny is to be seen. However, the internal war between the fear of being hurt and a call to be in high service was constant and consistent. I would make a decision to lay low, but the universe would call me out. When I was in middle school, I had two experiences that will describe the two sides of this inner struggle...

The announcement came out when I was in eighth grade. There was going to be a posture contest. Somehow, I was invited to participate. I was reluctant because we had to wear a swimsuit. My mother promised to help me pick the perfect one. So, we went shopping and a beautiful yellow one-piece caught my eye. It fit perfectly with one exception: I was flat chested and the bra cup sank in. The saleswoman convinced my mother that we needed a small insert. I wasn't convinced, because there was a distinct difference in the look of my chest and how it looked in this swimsuit. Both women said I looked great. So, I gave in.

The day of the contest came and I walked out on the stage. I was poised and had to admit that I felt pretty. I stood. I walked. I turned and the room cheered. Clearly, I was a hit. They lined us up and began to announce the winners. The teacher smiled and said, "and the grand champion is Cynthia James." I couldn't believe it. Even with the false breast inserts. I was elated. Maybe it was okay to be seen.

That swimsuit became my badge of acceptance. So, of course, I would want to go to the beach and show off. I lived in Minneapolis, where there is a myriad of lakes. I wanted to go to Calhoun Beach because it was the place where all the cool people went. I laid my blanket down. I strolled out to the water and waded in. I knew how to swim. Swimming was required in our school. However, I didn't want to rush in. I wanted people to see how fabulous I looked. Finally, the water got up to my waist and I did my best casual but elegant sidestroke out into the water. I was poetry in motion. Then, I dove down beneath the surface and when

I came up from being submerged, both inserts popped out of my suit and floated away from me. I tried to get them before anyone could see, but it was too late. People around me began to laugh. There was no way to pretend they weren't mine. I was mortified. The more I tried to get them, the more they slipped away. Finally, I got both and stuffed them back in so I could swim back to shore. People giggled as I picked up my blanket and walked away with my head bowed.

It seemed like it took forever to live down that experience. It probably would have gone away sooner if I had been able to laugh at it, but I couldn't. The entire experience just anchored in my consciousness that I was a victim, and being visible only brought pain. It took many years for me to understand that I am here, and we are all here, to shine and share our unique gifts.

You are here to shine your light

Have you ever thought about the fact that there would absolutely be no reason to be on the earth if you didn't have a purpose? I mean, what would be the point of being here and being invisible?

Mary is a CFO. She handles the money flow of her family's very successful company and has been a significant force in creating that success. However, her brother is the CEO, and has a dominant personality. He is a visionary and loves to be creative. When the company was created, the agreement was that they were equal. However, his imposing presence pushes things through without her input. When she speaks about it, she is told that "it wasn't important or he would have brought her into the conversation."

She is sitting in my office, very upset. She is afraid to blow up the business and/or her family by going to war with her brother. She had made an inner decision that she had no power; therefore, she didn't. Our work was to re-establish a knowing that she had a voice and deserved to use it.

By the end of our session, she had discovered a sweet seven-year-old "inner child." She remembered a day with her father. She was excited that she had been acknowledged for having the best project in her class. She had even beaten her brother. Her father told her she was not to boast and make her brother feel bad. It was that day she made the decision that she could not outshine her brother.

The next few months, we concentrated on the fact that her presence and brilliance was essential, and her voice was necessary to the company. It took some time to change the dynamic, but she created a new relationship with her brother based on equality and respect.

A POWERFUL MARKETING PRESENCE

It was time to look at my marketing. I had done pretty well but, when I sat down to look at my materials, I felt scattered. One person had created the cards. Another person had done the promo cards, and yet another had created the website. I had done it that way because money was a challenge. So, whenever I got money, I created a new marketing piece. That process had served me well, but it was time to create more cohesive materials.

I knew I needed to up-level my website since more and more people were discovering businesses through their web pages. Customers no longer wanted me to mail them media kits. People wanted to buy products from one place and not toggle around the Internet. They also wanted to get information quickly.

When I spoke to a couple of webmasters about my site, they said it was "nice." I didn't want "nice." I wanted wonderful. Each one asked me to explain how I wanted to be presented. They asked a lot of questions that left me feeling perplexed. It became clear that if I didn't know who I was, people would come to the website and be confused.

I took myself through a process of clarity, which took some time, primarily because the website, cards and brochures all had to have the same message. I am an energy person, and I wanted people to be excited by the message, the color and the vibration they experienced with any of my materials.

I went back to my mission statement and the work I had done before related to creating the life I wanted. I re-examined everything. Then, I honed it down to this:

Why: I feel ignited when I can support people in bringing their greatness to the planet.

Who: seekers and Thought Leaders, especially women, who play bigger in the world.

How: teaching, training, speaking, coaching.

Methods: Emotional Integration, music, creativity.

I worked with my designers, social media team member and assistant so that we were all on the same page.

When I finally went back to the web-designer, I was able to share what I wanted to say and whom I wanted to say it to. I had done my research on what made a great website. I requested that we look at each area together.

1. Appearance—meaningful graphics, great colors, professional photography.
2. Content—valuable, credible, original, well-organized, interactive.
3. Functionality—automation, tracking, powerful links.
4. Website Usability—easy to read and navigate, security.
5. Search Engine Optimization—easy for people to find me.

I was told that one of the goals of a website is to have great domain authority. I wasn't sure what that was, but then I looked it up. Here is what it said when I Googled the name:

Domain Authority is a measure of the power of a domain name and is one of many search engine ranking factors. Domain Authority is based on three factors: age, popularity, and size.

The search engines want to provide users with website results that can be trusted.

» Domain age is an indicator of trust because it proves to the search engines that the website has longevity and is a trusted source.

» Domain popularity is measured in part by the number of inbound links from quality sites that a domain has and information worth sharing.

» The size of a website on a domain contributes towards its authority because the number of pages that exists on a domain correlate with the amount of content that can generate inbound links. A larger website with quality content on each page will have more inbound links than a smaller website.

Domain authority, or domain trust, is important because it will help new pages of content (including blog posts) get indexed more quickly and have a better chance of ranking prominently in the search results.

My domain authority number today is 39. I am told that this number is very good and, any time I choose to change my website, my goal is to maintain this number and grow it.

TO DO OR NOT TO DO—SOCIAL MEDIA

I am a baby boomer, and many boomers witnessed technology move into our lives in unexpected ways. Suddenly, writing by hand was replaced with emails, smartphones, Ipads and various mobile devices. We watched as the schools replaced teaching the students cursive handwriting with typing on computers. Yet I remember taking such pride in writing and getting A's on my homework for my beautiful handwriting. Many of the young people I coach today have no idea about handwriting, and feel it is much faster to just use technology.

In a teen workshop I taught, I asked the students to write a letter to their future self. They were to address the envelope to themselves and also put their return address on the envelope. Several of them needed help because they had never written or mailed a letter. This amazed my teaching assistants.

Some of us have been open to exploring these new areas of communication. Others are appalled at how our ability to connect in person is being replaced. I cannot tell you how many people say things to me like, "What is the point of social media?" "I get all of my clients from referrals." "I am not interested in what people had for breakfast." "I don't have time to sit in front of a computer all day." I totally get why they feel this way, but when I decided to expand my brand in the world, something in me knew I had better learn to use the new media platforms.

At first, I fumbled around. I created a personal Facebook account and accepted *everyone* who asked to be a friend. About a year later, I got on Twitter and LinkedIn. I had no idea what purpose either of them served. I didn't even know that they had different audiences and purposes; I just did what I saw others doing.

When I wanted to share a project or new product, I posted. Most of the time, the results were minimal. Then, I hired someone who loved social media to support me. This was nice, and we created lovely graphics, but it did not grow my business.

Finally, I decided to take a social media class with my assistant. That one day was life-changing. Our instructor showed us the difference between each platform and helped me decide where to focus my attention. I also got clear that I needed someone whose passion was social media. I hired that woman to help me achieve my goals. Since that time, my presence in the world has accelerated. My growth in social media has gone up over 35% and continues to grow. Here are the benefits I receive:

» New clients find me through social media.

» My videos consistently get shared, which builds audience.

» People engaging with me on social media become part of my community.

» Collaborators follow me and become partners in ventures.

BRING YOUR VISIBILITY TO LIFE EXERCISE

If your business and your message were a pie, how might you want to slice it to serve your public? I believe the PIE should be sliced into three major areas. Take some time to sit down and write out how you want your marketing to be revealed in each area.

Promote—Where do you want to promote? How do you want people to feel when they see your promotions? What is the value of what you are promoting that will serve people and their needs?

Inform—What kind of information do you provide to help people overcome their challenges? How do you want to deliver this information? How many different ways can you inform people with different styles of learning?

Engage—How do you want to interact with the people who follow you? What kinds of tools do you need to engage people on different levels? How do you want to provide high touch and low touch to your clients?

I am in business to **A**ccess to a larger audience; **A**ccentuate the gifts I bring and offer them in great service to others; and **A**uthentically invite people to know who I am and what I stand for.

How do you want to be more visible in the world?

EXPANDING MY VISIBILITY

• • • • •

—Christy Belz

Why have you come to earth, do you remember? Why have you taken birth, why have you come? To love, serve and remember.

—Paramhansa Yogananda

I am starting to remember.

I have always known I have something to say, gifts to share, a message; yet, I have never felt certain of my place or my role here on the planet. There have even been days that I was not even sure I wanted to be here.

I had an interesting entrance and a challenging journey as a child...

I was the fourth baby born into a newly-opened hospital in the early morning hours. Of course, I do not remember my actual arrival. I surmise that the events that followed that morning are evidence of the truth that I have held most of my life: life is hard and I am not sure I want to be here.

As the story goes, I was separated at birth from my mother, a situation I truly do not understand. Why do we take a child who has been seeded, grown, nurtured and ejected from its only known source into a bright, cold world, and immediately take the child away from that source? Primal, I would suggest, and yet we still practice this today. Anyway, that day, as I lay in my bed away from my mother, my umbilical cord clamp came loose and I started hemorrhaging.

"Thank God the night nurse was making the rounds and found you!" as my mother tells it. Yeah, thank God, I think...now. Yet, I believe that moment was my answer to *Why have I taken birth, why have I come?*

Making one's way from incarnate to planet earth must be quite a journey. The forgetting of what happens when we leave the realm of spirit and make our way into a human body is full of mystery and awe. Yet, the feelings in this thing called life in its human form can be too much: too much pain; too much suffering; too much speed; too much information; too much feeling, emotion, trauma and sadness. It is just too much. That feeling fed my internal beliefs that I am a misfit, I don't fit in, and I am too sensitive to be here.

Most would never imagine this to be true about me. From what they see, I live an amazingly good life afforded few, and I have been blessed with health, wealth, loving friends and family. Yet, I often live in the question: what is this journey about? This wonder and questioning has led me here, today, to this paper, this pen—to start to share my answers to this question. To share my remembering of why I have come to earth— my awareness and assurance of something more—ME! My Essence.

I feel a deep knowing that it is time. This is the place to stop, and to start to face my fears of the unknown, my self-doubt, the "who do you think you are?" voice in my head. It is time to write and to share—to fully express ME, the truth, the vulnerability and authentically ME.

Yes, I am scared. Born and raised in the state of Kansas, I am big fan of the beautiful story *The Wizard of Oz*. My favorite character is the cowardly lion. I call on his archetype often with the mantra "A little courage, please." *Hello Courage* is the saying that I see each day as I walk into my workspace.

I have been scared for much of my life: scared of the uncertainty, scared to be vulnerable, scared of violence; fearful of the unknown and being made the fool. The fear and discomfort that I didn't fit in, wasn't smart enough, good enough or pretty enough. Yet, I know now that living in fear has not served me. It has kept me seemingly safe and very small.

Guillaume Apollinaire so beautifully illustrates this fear in the following passage:

"Come to the edge," he said.

"We can't, we're afraid!" they responded.

"Come to the edge," he said.

"We can't, we will fall!" they responded.

"Come to the edge," he said.

And so they came.

And he pushed them.

And they flew.

Today, I stand on the edge, not knowing what is "out there" beyond my own world, created by these fears and uncertainties; the paradigm of my life created by experiences and the stories I created about them. I have only been able to see through the limited lens of this view until now.

I know there is more - more of me, my Essence. The journey to this place of unknown and unexplored will take me in the direction I am called in, called by something bigger than me, much wiser than me.; as the song says, "To love, serve and remember."

To surrender into this place and fully give my faith and trust to source has not been easy. There are days when surrender is hard and humbling. I find myself caught yet again in the web of old thinking and untrue thoughts about myself and others. It is with conscious awareness, courage and willingness to explore new ideas and ways of seeing and believing that I find myself here and now.

Today, I walk down a different street. I am here to take a chance, to share me, and to invite those of you who are reading this to consider your own journey. I believe - I know - just like in the Wizard of Oz, there is a place, a home for each of us where we belong, where we are loved unconditionally. Where we are seen, heard, valued, appreciated and adored. This place is in me, and it is in you.

My life purpose is to continue to explore and expand my awareness of this inner place - this inner power - for myself, and to continue to share and help others on their inner journey.

Let's begin. Come to the edge...remember...breathe deep...take a step...

1, 2, 3, Jump! Let's fly together.

CHAPTER SEVEN

YOU CAN'T DO IT ALONE

• • • • •

No matter what accomplishments you make, somebody helped you.

—Althea Gibson

The strength of the team is each individual member. The strength of each member is the team.
—Phil Jackson

It is interesting to me that so many people in society do not want to and will not ask for help. There is this misguided thought that we should know how to do things or be able to figure it out on our own. We move into some weird sense of magical thinking that the solution to any problem lives inside our mind, and our only job is to access the information. We forget that every successful person had some semblance of a team. Hey, the Lone Ranger had Tonto and Silver. He was not a hero all by himself.

Part of this challenge is based on the growing experience of isolation in our culture.

Shankar Vedantam wrote an article in *The Washington Post* on June 23, 2006. The article shared, "Americans are far more socially isolated today than they were two decades ago, and a sharply growing number of people say they have no one in whom they can confide, according to a comprehensive new evaluation of the decline of social ties in the United States." That isolation and the need to appear perfect has caused people to sink inside themselves and cling to the belief that they must do it alone.

The work I do with clients is focused on getting them to become clear that NO ONE can manifest success on their own. We have to learn to trust our intuition and "play well with others." It is essential to understand that the diversity of thoughts, ideas and creative expression can manifest in powerful ways to reach our goals.

I used to think that I would appear stupid if I admitted that I didn't know or understand something. I think that belief, coupled with my deep desire to grow, fueled me to become an eternal student. At one time in my life, I was in school nine out of ten years before it dawned on me that perhaps I should get out into the world and practice.

I have a great and creative mind, so it has been easy to get clear on goals, move into action and bring form to my ideas. I would get an idea, create a deadline, research the process and get moving. I didn't believe I had enough money to invest in help, so I would just leap out and do it myself. That process worked. I created two books, 5 meditation CDs, five music CDs and numerous workshops. However, even with all my passion and education, I made huge mistakes that cost me time and money. Why? I didn't want to ask for help. Today, I use the lessons learned as part of my process to nurture clients into focus and collaborative ways of operating.

THE RIGHT TEAM MAKES ALL THE DIFFERENCE

When I decided to wake up and bring on team members, everything changed. That was the good news. I saw effective teams and realized that, with help, I could expand and create a more sustainable business model.

The challenge was that I looked at bringing in team members based on money and likeability. I had a budget, and they had to fit into that modest framework. It was also important how much I felt connected to them when we met. I knew better than to take people at face value; I had worked in human resources. But somehow, my training was overruled by my limited thinking. This proved to be a recipe for disaster.

Many people follow me and love what I do in the world. They want to support me and be in my presence. They are charismatic and likable human beings who really want to make a difference. That sounds like it should be a perfect partnership...but it was not.

There is an old adage that "you get what you pay for." That proved to be true for me. When I would interview people, I would tap in and see if I felt like there was a resonance. I listened for their passion in a particular area. Many who came were excited that they were self-taught and were able to learn quickly. If they had reasonable skills and were enthusiastic about their vision for my work, I considered them. I figured that I could teach them my system, and we would grow together.

What I forgot is that I move VERY fast, and anyone working with me has to be a quick processor and be self-motivated. I needed people who are proactive and that I didn't have to micro-manage. What ended up happening is that I was doing my job and their work, too. Because they lacked experience in supporting an author/speaker in the world, they often relied on me to support them. They also knew that the work was emotional integration, and would often expect me to process their emotional states of being. I ended up coaching and counseling them, and whining to my friends about not having the support I needed. Then,

I would agonize about letting them go and release them, oftentimes in ways that were painful.

One day, a dear friend said, "You are getting what you paid for. You have not called in excellence and expertise. You called admirers and cheap labor." Ouch. That hurt, but it was true. I wanted a mini-me, and I hired people who were incapable of supporting me in the world in the ways I needed. Let me be clear here: each person, in every arena, helped me get to where I am today. They saw me and wanted to be a part of the unfolding vision. I am grateful for their willingness to travel the path of my growth. However, and it is hard to admit, my fears and lack of consciousness didn't support any of us.

HERE IS WHAT I LEARNED:
» Passion for something does not make people skilled.
» Experience in the area you are hiring supports longevity.
» Hiring people who lack skill costs you money in the long run.
» Letting people go who have bonded with you emotionally is not easy.
» People can feel disappointed and angry when you ask them to step up in ways that point out their inadequacies.
» Setting up boundaries and expectations at the beginning creates clarity.
» Job descriptions (even for virtual or part-time people) are essential.

DON'T BE AFRAID TO DELEGATE
Most people I know don't want to admit that they are controlling. The will tell you that they like to make sure that things are in order.

I once asked a client who was feeling depleted and overwhelmed if she was asking for help. She was overworked in her job, taking care of her aging parents and nurturing family members and friends. She very quickly said, "No, I need to know that it is done right."

When I asked if she thought that this need to control might be the cause of her fatigue, she simply stated that she had always done it this way. Frankly, I could relate. I am clear how I want things done, and sometimes it is easier to do it myself rather than ask for help or teach someone else. The challenge with that train of thinking is that "doing it all" leaves very little time to engage in living a purpose-driven life. No matter what we may think, we can only do so much before the mind and body cease to function in optimal ways.

The word delegate comes from the Latin root *delegatus*. It means to give a task to someone or to assign something to someone. Think of delegating as taking things off of your plate and giving it to someone you trust. Effective delegation strengthens your position and ability to thrive. It also helps people grow and provides you with more time to focus on higher priority programs and projects.

TIPS FOR DELEGATION

» Look at the scope of your activities. Can any of them be eliminated or delegated?

» Explore the talents and skill sets of your people.

» Invite the employee to be honest about their ability to complete this work. What support do they need to succeed?

» Give people entire projects in their area of expertise rather than tasks. It supports accountability and engagement.

» Define what outcome is needed clearly.

» Be specific about what is expected and the timelines attached to this performance.

» Be very clear about the boundaries of authority that go with the delegated job.

- » Expect the employee to succeed.
- » Invite the employee to bring creative ideas on how to establish more efficiency.
- » Get clear on how you will measure progress.
- » Don't take the project back. Help the person learn how to be successful.
- » Have frequent feedback meetings to ensure ongoing success.
- » Understand that people can make mistakes when they are learning. What is the process for correction?

GREATNESS THRIVES IN AN ALIGNED TEAM

I loved the book *Good to Great* by James C. Collins. His five-year research of companies that moved from effective to extraordinary says that the secret sauce is having the right people in the right seats on the bus.

If you excel by doing what you love and what you are great at doing, why wouldn't you want your team members to do the same? I have worked for corporations and faith-based communities. Often times they hire and/or promote based on resumes, the need to cut costs or the need to keep people because they are loyal to the organization. Here is the interesting thing: if people are not passionate about what they do, they will under-deliver and become lackluster in engagements.

There are statistics that tell us that 29% of workforce employees are engaged, 45% are not engaged and 26% are actively disengaged. I believe that latter two exist because people are not excited to go to work and share from a place of passion and enthusiasm. That would not be the case if they were invited to bring their highest energy, skill and joy to the workplace.

Whether you are hiring within an organization or to support yourself as an entrepreneur, you want involved and committed people working for you.

I am going to encourage you to never settle for less than you deserve where employees are concerned. Wait for the right person. Offer them the opportunity to be part of a masterful team of people dedicated to making a difference and being in high service. Give them their marching orders and then turn them loose to bring their brilliance to your world. Then, have consistent team meetings where people share their wins, thoughts, ideas, concerns and revelations. You will discover that this team of people will be game changers in your business.

By the way, the team can start small. I know a woman who started with one assistant working out of her small home office. Today, that employee is still there, managing the administration for a multi-million-dollar company. She thrives on supporting her boss, the employees and the organization. In return, the company has a model of excellence and fulfillment in that employee.

Wherever you are in the process, take a breath and claim your greatness. Then go out and find the people who can help you make it happen.

DREAM TEAM EXERICSE:

Sit down and brainstorm, contemplate and journal. Write out the needs for your dream team. Be specific. You cannot dream too big. Use this as a guideline:

» What kind of skillset do I desire?

» What kind of experience is preferable?

» What kind of education is needed?

» What are the values of this employee?

» How does this person accomplish things, and does it match my style of working?

» How does this person process information and communicate with me?

» How does this person interact with me, my family and my clients?

» How will this person's vision support my vision?

» What is the abundant consciousness of the person I want to hire?

Now, write out an affirmative statement about this person or people in your life. Declare and claim how they show up, commit and deliver. Here is an example:

I am so excited to work with my assistant. This person is conscious, committed and willing to always bring their best. Integrity, conscious communication and excellence are foundational values for this person. They are connected to the vision of my work, are proactive and have a deep desire to live an abundant life. Conflict is handled in transparent and conscious ways. This person is always looking for ways to be more efficient. They deliver work before it is due, and are excited to do things to make my life easier. My clients, family and friends feel seen and honored whenever there is an interaction with this person. We grow together, and our working together is joyous and expansive for us both.

THE WISEST ADVISOR AND GREATEST POWER TOOL

* * * * *

—Liz Wendling

When I embarked on the journey of entrepreneurship, I believed I was capable of building my empire without the help of others. I thought I could do anything I set my mind to, and needed no one on the road to success - Oh, how wrong I was. My stinking thinking was leading me head-first into the entrepreneurial ditch. I discovered that *thinking* was completely different than *knowing*. So, I set out on a voyage to stop permitting my thinking (my head) to tell me what to do, and start trusting my body (my intuition) to expertly navigate me. The voyage would only be 18 inches long (the distance from my head to my body), but would prove to be transformational.

I have an education and formal business training. That training was focused on looking *outside* myself. I had little training on how to look *inside*. Learning how to understand and interpret my gut feelings, thoughts and hunches would be a powerful lesson as an entrepreneur.

Intuition is my greatest business tool and serves as a wise and perceptive guide. Turns out, I had my very own personal navigation system, brilliantly installed at conception that would help me on my journey.

At first, I had no clue how to tap into my intuition's incredible powers. I had no one to teach me how to use that power. When my intuition tried to guide me, I ignored it. When it attempted to warn me, I tuned it out. How many times have you had a gut feeling that something wasn't right, but you ignored it? Then, you said, "I knew I should have listened," or "I knew that was going to be a mistake." We need to be aware of that voice inside and what it's trying to tell us.

What benefits could be obtained by enhancing your ability to follow your intuitive voice? Consider your body. Some people decide to fine-tune their bodies through discipline, commitment and willpower. They eat right, exercise and turn their bodies into well-oiled machines that run smoothly and efficiently. Other people are content with the way their bodies are; they have a body that works fine the way it is. They think, "if it isn't broken, don't fix it." They choose to let the body do its job without a tune-up; an occasional look under the hood is enough for them. Similarly, consider your intuition. You can do the work to improve your intuition's performance, or you can let it come out now and then: your choice.

Today, my intuition is like a finely-tuned instrument. It's a gift for which I'm deeply grateful. My intuition is like a muscle—the more I use it, the more developed it becomes. You have that same capacity. You can choose to develop it or let it atrophy. But, if you want your business to grow and your life to change for the better, listen to and use your intuition. It will guide you to the right people and partners to grow your business and your life.

My natural knowing is spot-on. After meeting with or talking to anyone about the possibility of partnering and working with them, I would use a simple and powerful technique. This technique would guide me to the right answer. I would ask myself if the situation felt light or heavy. Was it expanding or contracting? Did I feel joyful or gloomy? Did I want to jump up and say *heck yes* or run away with a *hell no*? Feelings don't lie. I knew I was being guided to what was best and right for me.

Your inner navigation system guides you to do exactly what you need to do and steers you away from life's roadblocks, barriers and construction zones, which slow you down and trip you up. Is your intuition turned on? Do you even know where the "on" switch is?

Some women I work with or interact with in business keep their navigation systems turned off. Sometimes their systems are turned on, but the volume is turned way down. Not using this internal device and following its guidance makes your road to success a constant construction zone. Potholes, roadblocks, floods, detours, traffic jams and fender benders can be avoided when you turn on and use your internal navigation system.

During my life's business journey, I wish I had turned on and tapped into my friendly inner voice and heard, *turn around, you missed a great opportunity back there. Be prepared for a huge detour up ahead. Stop— major setbacks coming your way. Danger ahead if you go in that direction. Steer clear of that business deal.*

We are all fully equipped with an internal guidance system factory-installed at conception that will direct us on a path that is well-lit and well-marked. But, to be able to hear the voices, nudges and advice that guide us along the way, we must turn on and use our internal navigation system.

CHAPTER EIGHT

FINANCIAL FREEDOM IS OBTAINABLE

. . . . .

You can make EXCUSES and earn SYMPATHY, OR You can make MONEY and earn ADMIRATION. The choice is always yours.

—Manoj Arora

If you create incredible value and information for others that can change their lives, and you always stay focused on that service, the financial success will follow.

—Brendon Burchard

Let's talk money. I know it is a tender subject. Many of us prefer to speak about abundance. I am all for that but, in this moment I prefer to get real. Let's discuss our relationship with finances. I don't know about you, but this has been an area of deep exploration for me. I come from humble and poor beginnings. My entire family was focused on survival, and the lack of money was always an issue. *How are we going to pay* bills? *Don't you know money doesn't grow on trees? Don't you understand that money is the root of all things evil? Are you trying to drive me to the poorhouse?* These kinds of questions flooded our conversations and family discourses. The underlying message was that we did not have enough because there was not enough. Someone or something was withholding, cheating us, or refusing to pay what we were worth.

I was always ashamed of our financial situation. I was jealous of the girls in my school wearing great clothes, shoes and handbags. I wanted to be included, but it was clear that I was poor and not a good fit with the popular girls. I decided that I needed to achieve to be accepted. If I didn't have money, I would be embraced because I was talented, smart, charismatic and engaging. Achieving this was not easy since I was really shy at the core of my being. All I knew was that I had to get out of the ghetto and make something of myself. If that meant changing my personality, so be it. I sang in the talent shows. I was elected to office in high school. I was on debate and chess teams and I took French. This strategy worked while at school. At night, I went home to our modest apartment and/or house of the moment and watched my mother work to the point of exhaustion just to make ends meet.

I didn't understand visualization at that time, but that is exactly what I did as a young woman. I saw myself traveling around the world. I told people I was going to sing on international stages. I dreamed of being a renowned actress and a singer. I saw myself living a life of luxury and being supported in extraordinary ways, even though it made no logical sense. My friends and family told me to stop daydreaming and deal with my reality. I was told that no child on welfare was going to live that kind of life, so I stopped talking about it - but I kept dreaming.

When those dreams started to manifest, I simply smiled when my family told me that my life was miraculous. Yes, I flew around the world as a flight attendant with Trans World Airlines. I lived in New York and hung out with celebrities. Over a period of 20 years, I created an acting and singing career that paid me well, married an affluent man, continued to travel the world, owned property in Los Angeles, cared for my mother, grandmother and children and lived a bountiful life. But, here is the rub: I still felt poor.

I believe that my clients are a reflection of where I am or where I have been. So, it is no surprise that many of my women clients struggle with this challenge. Even the ones who have successful businesses find themselves in constant states of worry about having enough, continuing to flourish and establishing a retirement fund that will sustain them when working long, strenuous hours is no longer desirable.

The interesting thing is that women are earning, spending, and influencing spending at a greater rate than ever before. Statistics tell us that women account for $7 trillion in consumer and business spending in the United States and, over the next decade, they will control two-thirds of consumer wealth. Women make or influence 85% of all purchasing decisions and purchase over 50% of traditional male products, including automobiles, home improvement products and consumer electronics. So, why are we so challenged with creating and sustaining wealth?

Money, when used as an instrument of great service, is a powerful tool. I have learned that money is just energy and, when used in a conscious way, is transformative. Our relationship to money is always the issue.

WHEN IS IT ENOUGH?

It is 1989 and I am sitting in my room. I am alone and it is very quiet. I am sitting on the edge of the bed and in my lap is a huge, oversized check for $100,000. I have just won the TV show *Star Search* in the acting category. Millions of people saw Ed McMahon hand me the check. You would think that I would be excited and filled with joy; instead I felt isolated. No family and friends were around to lift me up, even though there had been plenty the night before at my celebration party.

This was a powerful manifestation moment. I had written a check to me from the universe 5 years earlier. I put the check on the wall in my bathroom and looked at it daily. Now, I was $100,000 richer. However, the only thing I could think about was, "What's next?" How could I be conscious with the money? What if I blew it? How was I going to leverage this win? I had the presence of mind to know that this was an old-paradigm inner dialogue. I had experienced many of these conversations in my mind, and they oftentimes led to depression. I picked up the phone and called a dear friend, who was a spiritual counselor.

"Are you aware that you often do this?" he asked. "You don't seem to have the capacity to enjoy the moment." I sat quietly for what seemed like an eternity. I didn't like what he was saying, but I knew it was true. Then, he said, "Are you willing to do an exercise?" I agreed, and what he asked me to do was to walk around the house saying, out loud, "I am enough." Then, he told me to call him back when I felt at peace. I thought that it would be easy and that I would do the exercise and call him back within the hour.

That was not the case. The speaking of that simple statement brought up deep emotions and feelings of inadequacy. I spent hours sobbing, yelling and lying on my bed immobilized. Winning that money was just enough to put a glaring mirror in front of me that said, "I believe there will never be enough to make you feel whole."

We are witnessing extraordinary greed on the planet. The need to make money seems to supersede the care of the planet and/or humanity. Legislation has said that corporations are individuals and have the same rights. The "bottom line" has become a universal focus. In the meantime, global warming has reached critical levels. The middle class in many countries is shrinking. People are experiencing hunger all over the planet. Challenges with the lack of water are increasing. We talk about these things but often do not have strength, courage or knowledge to look at money through a different lens—as a way to be of service in resolving these problems.

We also have a vast number of people living beyond their means, buried by credit card debt and with no understanding of how to create wealth.

THE CORE DECISION

It is important to say here that we all have work to do in our lives. There is no "arrival place." We learn new things, grow and then are given opportunities to re-examine our core beliefs. Many people view me as rich and abundant. I do live an abundant life on every level, but that does not mean that I do not continue to look at my true relationship to money. I know that I must constantly re-examine my beliefs around finances when I start to become concerned.

My work with people is all about mind/body connection. If we learn the language of the body, we will have all the information we need to expand. That is because everything that has ever happened to us is encoded in the body.

I was sitting in a restaurant with a friend. He is a brilliant international consultant, and has done an enormous amount of work in the field of transformation. We were discussing a huge moment in his life where he was pushed to the edge. He was in a class, and was being asked to look at a core belief that had held him hostage in his life. He called it the **moment of decision**. What he discovered in that class was that his hidden core belief was that he was stupid. I was intrigued. I don't know many people smarter than this man. He told me how that moment had opened him up to a more expansive way of looking at his life and choices.

I began to share a conversation that I had with my coach. It was about my inability to ask for what I deserved in charging my clients. I told him about my work with people and that if we were to discover where this feeling lived in my body, it would be the heart. I felt enormously safe to share with this man, and told him that I felt clear that my heart could be a portal to my understanding in this area.

All of a sudden, in this busy restaurant, I had a memory of being a three-year-old child locked in a dark basement and told that the devil was going to get me. I remembered being terrified. As I shared the story, my heart area constricted and I said, "The decision I made in that moment was that I was alone and had to survive on my own." He sat with me quietly.

Then, something amazing happened: a still voice inside of me said "No, that is not the decision you made. You decided that you were meant to struggle." I spoke that thought out loud and began to cry. It was the truth. My entire existence had played out in the field of "struggle" and the need to struggle. I was an expert at overcoming odds to win. It had happened in business, in contests and in relationships. The way I won was to climb mountains of challenge. I moved in and out of the awareness that I was in a public place, having this vulnerable conversation. Somehow, the revelation was more powerful than my need to mask my emotion in this restaurant. I wiped my eyes with my napkin and he gently touched my arm with extraordinary compassion. It was a transformative moment. A wave of peace blanketed me. What if I was not intended to struggle? What if that lie had been an invisible rope around my neck my entire life?

HOW MUCH ARE YOU WILLING TO RECEIVE?

I have been a student of the law of attraction and building abundance for many years. I am clear that the life we are living is an exact mirror of our consciousness, especially where money is concerned. The universe, quantum field or the field of infinite possibilities, whatever you choose to call it, is always feeding back to us what is seeded. If you plant roses, you do not expect to get petunias. If you plant carrots, you do not expect potatoes. So, why is that we plant fears and doubts about money and expect abundance to miraculously appear?

There is also a law of circulation that says that we must give **and** receive. It is both that creates flow. Many of us are brought up hearing, "It is more blessed to give than to receive." Who made that up? It was probably some person or organization that wanted us to give to them.

Giving is essential, from my point of view. That is why so many religious and spiritual organizations promote tithing. The concept of giving "first fruits" came from an agricultural experience. Giving from your harvest supported the community or government, but also was a way of affirming that your abundance would continue because of your generosity.

In my life, there are two levels of activation where these laws are concerned. When I look back at my life, it is so clear that my world has always reflected expansion. I have lived in New York, and my life has been adventurous and joy-filled. What I have learned is that there must be give and take. There must be circulation in all areas of life. I cannot expect to receive abundance if I am not willing to give. For me, that means giving to places that feed my soul. I choose my spiritual community and organizations that are in alignment with my values. It doesn't matter what you choose; it is just important to choose.

Receiving is about a willingness to open and allow the universe to support and resource you. Abundance is all around us. I have never had a bird fly in my house and complain about not having enough food. Somehow, nature and the animal kingdom understand that they are resourced.

FINANCE EXERCISES

These contemplation questions are powerful tools to gain clarity about your current reality regarding finances. You can do one question at a time or use the questions below as a series in one sitting.

Sit quietly. Some people like to do this in silence, and others really like to have quiet music in the background. I encourage you to use paper or a journal. Write using a stream of consciousness technique. That means to write whatever comes to your mind. It does not have to make sense. Just let it flow. What you will discover is that the writing will override the monkey mind chatter and eventually drop into deeper spaces of awareness. I like to do this kind of work in the morning when I feel fresh. If this is an area you really want to explore, write every day for 30 days. What you will discover are hidden beliefs and fears that may have been holding you back. They are actually energy blockages. Here are some questions to spark your process:

What was my moment of decision about who I am and how I am treated in this life? What was that core decision?

Do I avoid dealing with finances and gaining clarity on my financial status? Why?

What is my current relationship to money?

Do I consistently overspend? What is the payoff?

Do I need to seek support with my finances? Why haven't I done that?

Am I ready for retirement? If not, why not?

Where am I regarding financial planning? What would support me?

MEDITATION ON FINANCIAL FREEDOM

This is the perfect moment to unleash your financial freedom. It is available for you. So, please sit back and close your eyes. Connect with your body and see how it feels as we enter the conversation of "financial relating and expansion." DON'T LOOK AT YOUR PAST, JUST WITNESS. THIS IS THE ONLY MOMENT YOU HAVE.

Breathe in gently and exhale easily. ALLOW YOURSELF TO RELAX with each exhale. This is your personal process and it will be done in the perfect way for you. As you do this process you may see images, hear sounds or just have feelings. It is all in alignment with what you need in this moment.

Continue to breathe.

Stand at the beginning of a path. Before you step onto the path... set an intention to be open and available for the gifts of this journey. Now, activate a willingness to go deep and to be honest in your ability to receive. Step onto the path.

As you walk, you will see three guides on the side of the road. Each has an envelope that contains significant amounts of money. Your only job is to surrender something to these guides.

THE FIRST GUIDE looks at you with love and says, "Can you give up SUFFERING?"

The envelope will support your freedom if you can do this one thing. If you can do it, the guide will hand you the envelope.

The guide continues, "If there is any part of you that is still attached to SUFFERING, I will honor you, but you cannot receive the gift I hold. I will hold this until you are ready to surrender and receive. If you are, truly in your heart, willing to release the entanglements with SUFFERING, take the envelope and put it in your pocket. If not, move on and know that I will hold the envelope in safe keeping until you are ready."

YOU MOVE TO THE SECOND GUIDE, and the guide smiles. "Can you give up ANGER AND RESENTMENT to receive this envelope? Take a moment and think if there is anyone or anything that still holds you hostage to anger and resentment. If you can give it up, I will give you this envelope."

"BE AWARE" said the guide, "THAT IF YOU WANT TO ARGUE FOR YOUR RIGHT TO BE UPSET OR JUSTIFY THESE FEELINGS, YOU ARE NOT READY. If you truly are free in this area, take the envelope. If not, know that I honor you and will keep the envelope until you are ready. You must be honest." This guide is connected to your heart.

Now, move to the third guide. It is a feminine form. "Will you give up THE NEED TO JUDGE YOURSELF AND OTHERS?" the guide asks. "Take a moment to become still and check in with yourself. ARE YOU JUDGING YOURSELF OR OTHER PEOPLE IN YOUR LIFE? If you are, I will not release the envelope."

Feel the love coming from the guide as she now says, "JUDGMENTS BLOCK YOUR FLOW. I am here to support your freedom. If you are free from judgment, I will give you this envelope. If not, know that we three guides will support your healing process."

Please honor yourself and notice where you can let go and where you cannot.

Now, please look back down the path and thank the three guides. They have nothing but love in their eyes. If you have received any envelopes, give thanks for your growth and willingness. If you didn't get an envelope, allow yourself to be grateful for the work you have done and the work you have yet to do.

Now acknowledge yourself for walking this path and, when you are ready, slowly walk back down the path. Breathe slowly and when you are ready...open your eyes.

Take some time to journal this experience and know that you can use this meditation as many times as you like in support of your financial freedom.

WHAT IS WEALTH?

. . . . .

—Kathleen Lenover

Let's begin with a high level recap of a wanderer's sojourn. The entrepreneur spirit was alive and well in my primary family. Dad demolished structures and Mom re-sold the used building materials. My two older brothers worked with Dad, and I helped Mom in this demolition and salvage operation. We filled in with "hilligans" from the remote hills of Kentucky, thus it was common for an employee who could not write, read, nor manage a banking relationship. Mom became the banker. That seemed so important to me that I never realized how poor we were.

Throughout this life of struggle, Mom always found a way to pay for Catholic school's tuition. There, I fell in love with the remarkable women who served us as teaching nuns. For 12 years that still, small voice within kept encouraging me to give their lifestyle a try. After graduation, I entered the Sisters of Charity of Cincinnati.

I loved being a teaching Sister. The vow of poverty was in total concert with my childhood experiences. The community was quite similar. That vow of poverty did not mean we were poor: it meant we lived frugally and owned nothing. All our needs were met. We just had to ask permission for a new tube of toothpaste. I now realize this was the foundation for understanding that God is my Source and I could trust in that.

The "call" to do a kind of work not possible as a Sister began to dominate my thinking. After 13 years, I left the Order in search of what that might be. That decision was more courageous than the one to enter the convent, because I didn't know what that call meant. Trust can be scary. There was no family or community to cover all the basics. How would God, as my Source, provide?

There I was in my thirties, and I felt like a teenager exploring what it meant to be a salaried employee. I had to find out how to open a checking and savings account; how to buy a car, license, and insurance; find an apartment; buy household furnishings. I had no interest in even learning about a will, life insurance, retirement planning, 401(k) options, etc. With a Masters' degree in Education, I could spell S-T-O-C-K- and B-O-N-D, yet I had absolutely no idea what those terms meant. This required growing up fast!

Networking helped me land a position providing financial information for teachers and non-profit employees. My teaching, counseling, love of learning and entrepreneur experiences were fully used. I loved it. That resulted in being one of the top three advisors repeatedly. I was using the American work ethic to the max. This was encouraged by the prevailing attitude that women had to constantly prove themselves in the workplace. I loved a song's lyric: "I am woman, watch me roar..." Balancing and honoring the left-brain, bottom line, testosterone-driven and competitive part of me with the right brain, nurturing, open and receptive counselor has been a life-long focus. It was a whole new world for me.

Success expanded in proportion to my education. To broker an account, I chose to earn multiple securities designations, including the Principal's license. In addition, I went after the creme de la creme Certified Financial Planner®. I was so proud to be a CFP® serving in the ranks of those (mostly) men who were pioneers in providing planning to that vast sea of Americans who had never been taught the basics of sound money management. Other designations and degrees quickly followed, some of which included Certified Financial Coach®, Estate

Planning Professional, Certified Senior Advisor, and multiple specialty insurance licenses.

What surprisingly crept in was the arrogance of success. Along with clients, my lifestyle expanded. I began noticing my impatience and judgment of frugality and simplicity. It sparked the inquiry regarding what is wealth vs poverty; an attitude of prosperity vs poverty thinking; and is an awareness of values the most important determinant of financial success?

I raised my minimums to serve those who needed them. My wealthy clients knew the answer to life's problems is not more money. Their lifestyles got large enough that some found peace of mind, and with others it diminished. Their tax burdens were daunting. For some, life became more about managing their assets and lifestyle while worrying about other's intentions for their friendship. They were less concerned about living freely and fully. We all began to wonder: when is enough, enough? Wherein lies sufficiency?

June 2013 was a watershed month. I sold my financial planning practice to a team of awesome advisors and graduated from seminary training with a Masters in Consciousness Studies. A new chapter began. God continues to be my Source. It's a delight to see how creative Spirit is in providing richness for my personal growth.

I hope you saw yourself somewhere in this story line. You are awesome, you are good enough, you deserve to be supported and you are worthy of all the self-care you choose. I love paraphrasing His Holiness, the Dalai Lama's belief that the world will be saved and it will *be at the hands of western women*. Welcome to that august assignment!

CHAPTER NINE

MASTERY AS POWERFUL PRESENTERS

· · · · ·

People don't buy what you do; they buy why you do it.
And what you do simply proves what you believe.

—Simon Sinek

I have always loved speaking. It wasn't always on a stage; I spent a huge majority of my time as a teenager on the phone. I had this fabulous pink princess telephone and I would lie on my bed and talk for hours. My mother would tell me to get off, so I would. I would hurry up to get my chores done and then get right back on the phone. At night, I would talk under the covers way past my bedtime.

I was shy, believe it or not, so, speaking in front of people was scary. Interesting, since I joined the debate team in high school. I think I really joined it because I wanted to be liked. I was not popular and felt like I needed to find a way to fit in. It was in the debate club that I blossomed. My mind was quick and I could take a concept and find interesting ways to argue my point. The teacher who supported the team told me that I had a gift and invited me to consider looking at becoming a lawyer. I laughed inside because there was no way my family could afford to send me to law school.

I was always excited to go with the team to competitions. I somehow found a way to get up in front of people and really create energy in the room. There weren't many who could stand up against me. I felt powerful, smart and engaging. At that time, I had no idea that this would become a part of how I would make a living. It just made me feel as if I was successful at something.

Throughout the years, this training has supported me in bringing my best to any stage, platform or relationship. My husband jokingly says it is obvious that I was a debater whenever we are in a disagreement and I am holding onto a position. I am clear about my points and focused on the outcome.

Becoming a public speaker came gradually into my life. It started with presentations in corporate America. Being an actress helped because I was comfortable on a stage. It was easy for me to memorize lines, so learning points for a presentation was effortless. I was working for a media management company and my boss supported several divisions. They were all doing pretty well, but not all were at the top of their game. There was one man, Steve, who got my attention. He was smart, driven and very charismatic. He also liked the way I managed my boss's office. He was interested in the fact that I was in school (at the time I was earning my spiritual counseling degree). One day, I read in the newspaper that some companies were opening to coaching, mindfulness training and spiritual support. I asked him if I could share with him what I was learning, and he was open. I did some exercises with him and he invited me to talk to his sales team. He was number two in his field and he wanted to be number one. I was nervous, but said yes.

After my work with his team, Steve's division had an amazing year. They became #1 and sales went up 37%. My boss asked me to do the same work with his other teams, and I was in heaven. What I found out was that I thrived being in front of people and teaching them how to be great at what they did.

FEEDBACK AS A GIFT

I was taking a class on speaking for ministers and felt very confident that this would be a breeze for me. By now, I had spoken at different events, taught a lot of classes and facilitated workshops. I got up to do my first talk. After one minute, the instructor stopped me. He said, "Why are you smiling?" I was a little stunned. I didn't even realize I was smiling, so I said nothing. He told me to start again, and I did. Once again he stopped me. He asked again, "Why are you smiling?" At that point, I was uncomfortable, so I said, "It feels right." He said, "No. You are smiling because you want us to like you. It is a gimmick." I was getting angry but stayed calm. Then, he said, "Why do you need us to like you?" I snapped back, "I don't. I am trying to give my talk and you keep interrupting." He looked me dead in the eye and said, "You can argue for your limitations or understand that I am trying to make you a better speaker." I took a breath and said "Go ahead." He continued by telling me I was a good speaker, but I was never going to be great if I didn't get away from trying to make people like my message and me. It was a hard moment, but it transformed my speaking. I gave the speech again with a clear intention of sharing why the topic was important to me. The people in the room told me that the speech then had depth and meaning. It was then I decided to never let my ego get in the way of feedback supporting my growth.

SPEAKING SHOULD BE JOYOUS

There are techniques that make a good speaker, and every speaking coach can tell you those off the top of their head. But, what makes a speaker **great** is bringing joy and passion to the stage. So, how do you do that?

1. **Approachability** – Can the audience relate to you and sense your vulnerability?

2. **Transparency** – Can you stand in knowing that your message is

powerful? When you can do that, you don't need to defend your position or hide who you are.

3. **Trustworthy Voice** – Can you speak from the heart with un-abashed freedom? You must bring your uniqueness to every speech.

4. **Humble Authority** – Can you bring your humility to the plat-form, letting people know that you are still learning?

5. **Authentic Humor** – Can you tell stories that make you human and everyone can relate to while laughing at yourself?

6. **Making a Difference** – Can you move people to change their perspective and, ultimately, their lives?

THE "WHY" OF YOUR MESSAGE IS WHAT PEOPLE WANT TO KNOW

Simon Sinek speaks very vividly about the importance of great leaders being extraordinarily clear about WHY they do what they do. To me that means getting to the core of what ignites you. This is important for everyone—it does not matter how or where you present yourself in the world. Get clear about why you want to do what you do, and everything else will fall into place.

I love being with people and supporting them in awakening to the possibilities that lie before them. Getting people to tap into the extraordinary essence that brings them alive and lights them up makes my heart sing.

Many years ago, I had a very distraught man come to me for help. He had "escaped" from a cult but felt lost, disconnected and disoriented most of the time. He was a musician and could find some semblance of center when he played music, but the rest of the time he had difficulties communicating and staying present.

Our first few months together were difficult. He had major trust and post-traumatic stress issues. So, closing his eyes and doing mind/

body work was almost impossible for him. He was afraid that he might lose himself if he let go. I remember thinking that I wasn't sure I could support him, but I kept affirming that I would be guided to do what was necessary for his highest good because I saw his beautiful essence.

The one place we could connect was when we talked about his music. Playing made him feel alive. So, we began to start our sessions connecting to the joy of sharing music. I would use music to teach him how to do brief meditations and centering processes. Slowly, we began to open the doors to the trauma he had experienced. Little by little he opened up.

One day, he came in very happy. I asked what was bringing him so much joy. He had gotten a part-time job playing music for people who were hospitalized. He was hired by a chaplain to support his program. My client couldn't stop talking about how he had connected with the heart of each person and played music he felt would support his or her health. The results were tremendous. The chaplain gave him more hours and he started to become more relaxed.

The interesting thing is how this impacted the rest of his life. He cleaned up his house. He connected more with people and could have clear conversations. He was booking more gigs playing music in different venues. He was also elated with his comfort in front of an audience. When I asked him how he thought he was doing, he said, "I am here to play music, and my music helps people heal. There is nothing more important to me." That was the moment I knew he had found his "why." At that point, we could start building his transformation on the foundation of his purpose.

MASTER SPEAKER EXERCISES

When you are creating and preparing to do a talk, there are some rules that will support you in being successful:

TALK CREATION TOOLS:

» CLEAR AND UNPRETENTIOUS MESSAGE – You want it to be easy for the audience to understand what you are saying. Keep it simple.

» USE NO MORE THAN 3 POWERFUL POINTS – You don't want your audience to be confused. What are the most important ideas you want them to walk away with?

» STORIES – Any story you tell should be about you, and should be from a place of vulnerability. People want to know that you are humble and have overcome things to get where you are. Create a toolkit of at least 10 powerful stories that will invite people to know you and why your message can support them.

» USE PHOTOS MORE THAN WORDS – If you are using Power-Point, find powerful photos and graphics. Let the visuals be the way you invite people into your message. You don't want your audience to read your presentation on a screen.

» REHEARSE, REHEARSE, REHEARSE – You want to walk on the stage with confidence because you are well-prepared. That way, it won't matter if there is a heckler or technical difficulty. You will be anchored in your material.

» WEAR YOUR POWER COLOR/OUTFIT – People make decisions about how you look and who you are the moment you step onto a stage. You want to be powerful, strong, beautiful and engaging before you speak. This is the time to get an expert to support your choices. You only have one time to create a first impression.

» CENTER BEFORE ENTERING THE STAGE – This can be a short meditation, body warm-up, breath work or prayer. What is important is that you do something to move you to your center. You want your mind to be clear and focused. You also want your body to look and feel relaxed.

CENTERING MEDITATION

Stand quietly, close your eyes and focus on your breath. Breathe in the word "peace" and breathe out the word "joy." Let the peace fill your body from head to toe. Let the peace you inhale bathe you and begin to spill out into the area around you. Breathe in the peace and exhale the joy so that both qualities move onto the stage and into the audience. You need only do this for 3-5 minutes. You are creating an inner joy and peace, and are consciously breathing that energy into the room where you will speak. This is a process that will support alignment, attunement and coherence with your audience.

◆

AUTHENTIC BRILLIANCE

. . . . .

— Jean Hendry

I am standing in the front of a room full of middle- and high-level executives. I'm teaching them how to be better at what they do, how to be excellent leaders by being more real, more vulnerable, more aware – more AUTHENTIC. I am really good at this, and I am making a difference for many of them. For the most part, they are wonderful people - people I really like; people who are trying to learn, become more, and do better work for themselves and their organization - work I know is incredibly important for them...

AND I AM ABSOLUTELY MISERABLE.

I am a fake, a hypocrite... my smile and my caring for these people is genuine, but my heart, my passion is nowhere to be found. *I am completely inauthentic in teaching them how to be authentic.* My stomach drops and my smile fades... I wonder if they can tell?

How in the world did I get here? The truth is, I've always known what I love to do. I played dress-up and make-up and read fashion magazines from the moment I could talk. I started telling people what they should wear when I was seven. I always knew what looked best on me and on everyone else, too! My mother used to say, in her Texas drawl, "Jeannie, I can't wait until you have your own boutique. People will come from all over."

But I didn't do it. You see, I was the "smart" kid, one of the few who left the small West Texas town where I grew up. I had big things to prove—

that I could make it in the world, make good money, make a contribution, make something of myself—and that didn't involve anything as frivolous as clothing or make-up or hair or how people present themselves. No, I needed to do something IMPORTANT.

I must admit, I was highly influenced by my perception of what others thought of me. My growing-up years were conditioned by the common societal opinion of what beautiful (tall, skinny, blonde—not me!), successful (confident, rich, high-powered—not me!) women were like. More dramatically, my "boutique-supporting" mama was mentally and emotionally ill, creating a yo-yo environment that left me severely deficient in the self-esteem department.

So, I made the decisions I thought I should, and built a façade of what I thought a successful woman looked like. (Although I had a lot of difficulty with the tall and blonde part...!) I got a business degree, married the right guy, and took a high-paying job with an international company selling technology products and teaching people how to improve their companies. After fifteen years of pretending I liked it, I left and went out on my own—consulting in a similar field because, after all, I had tons of experience in business and I couldn't possibly make money or have any impact doing what I really wanted to do. Right?!

There wasn't a single "aha!" moment for me. It was more like a slow death, an ever-increasing sense of numbness, a feeling of stepping into the abyss. I never felt successful in my business work, never felt like I'd "made it." The façade I'd built began to crumble—my marriage disintegrated, my business failed, and I was exposed. I know now that it's because I was never "all in;" my heart stayed behind, clinging to a different vision. I finally reached the point of no return, that place where the pain was so great that my only options were to choose my heart or burn in hell forever...

I've had to come to terms with my need to do "important" work. But when you pay attention to your heart, it's ALWAYS important. Here's what I now understand: my work is not about creating a façade, dressing up your outside to follow the latest trend, or look like someone in a magazine: my work is about connecting to the heart, to what's unique about you, to what I call your **Personal Brilliance**. And once we've uncovered what that is for you, I can teach you how to best present yourself to our visual world in a way that is congruent with your best self. I call it, "embracing your inner brilliance and aligning your outer brilliance."

How do I know this is the right work for me? Because my heart swells when I do it – I can hardly keep it in my chest. When a woman tells me that I'm a "professional *seer* because I see her beauty from the inside out," or that she's "found a new level of personal expression and self-confidence" because of our work together, it's hard for me not to cry. Not because the accolades make me feel "important," but because my gifts helped her see the beauty that she truly is and support her in showing up more powerfully in her world.

My journey has only begun. Every day I get the opportunity to choose me, and I don't always get it right. But the difference between a numb heart and a full one is unmistakable—and that's how being authentic feels.

CHAPTER TEN

BUILDING COMMUNITY THROUGH POWERFUL PARTNERSHIPS

• • • • •

As you navigate through the rest of your life, be open to collaboration. Other people and other people's ideas are often better than your own. Find a group of people who challenge and inspire you, spend a lot of time with them, and it will change your life.

—Amy Poehler

Our willingness to acknowledge that we only see half the picture creates the conditions that make us more attractive to others. The more sincerely we acknowledge our need for their different insights and perspective, the more they will be magnetized to join us.

—Margaret J. Wheatley

Communication creates partnerships.

—Jada Pinkett Smith

You will accelerate your process if you have powerful partnerships. There are people or organizations you can recognize right away as places to support you or your business. Others might take more effort because trust can happen over time.

My business partner, Jean, is the perfect example. I met her twelve years ago, and something in me felt instantly attracted to her energy and brilliance. I invited her to lunch and, during a conversation at the table, I told her, "I don't know where or when, but we are going to work together." Let me say here that she is a very bright and structurally-minded business-woman, and I am a highly expressive creative. At first look, we are quite different. At that lunch, Jean looked at me and I could tell she was trying to find a way to be nice but thought that I was a little out of my mind. I was just as clear that she just had not caught the vision and, when she did, we were going to build something amazing.

In the last six years, she has helped me create my certified coaching program, the Women Creating Our Futures online mastermind series and conferences, and co-hosts my live events. We also co-created VIP experiences for clients wanting to go to the next level and build their platform visibility.

Even though we appear to be very different, we create a "whole brain" operation. Our collaboration and ability to honor each of our gifts has brought great benefit to us, individually and collectively.

EVERY HERO HAD SUPPORT FROM SOMEONE

I believe that collaboration and partnerships help us move forward in the world. Trying to "do it all alone" seems like a lot of work. It can find us spinning our wheels and feeling stuck.

I was thinking about super heroes. Often times, there is one that looks like the hero. However, there is always someone supporting them in the world. For example:

» Superman had Lois Lane and Jimmy

» Wonder Woman had Hippolyta and Steve Trevor

» James West had Artemus Gordon

» Iron Man had War Machine

» Captain America had Bucky

Just because you have a powerful vision doesn't mean the message will get to the right people. In 2012, there was something called the Venus Transit. A **transit of Venus** across the sun takes place when the planet Venus passes directly between the sun and a superior planet, becoming visible against (and hence obscuring a small portion of) the solar disk. During a transit, Venus can be seen from Earth as a small black disk moving across the face of the sun. There are many astrologers and cultures that believe a transit brings great power to the planet that can be used to accelerate our personal expansion. This is primarily because these events happen rarely in a lifetime.

I decided to do a tele-series using the Venus Transit as a backdrop. The only way to get people involved in the series and attend was to ask for help. So, I invited great speakers, teachers and authors to talk about how we can use this time to create more powerful lives.

I was told to create an **affiliate** and/or **joint venture** program. An affiliate program is a marketing program where you can receive commission for helping a parent company. A joint venture (JV) is a business agreement in which the parties agree to develop, for a finite time, a new entity and new assets by contributing equity. They exercise control over the enterprise and consequently share revenues, expenses and assets.

I invited my expert guests to share the tele-series with their mailing lists. I was charging for the series, so I asked these guests to share in the profits. Everyone that signed up under their code brought them income, and also brought me income. It was a win/win for us all. That one act brought over 8,000 people to the series and supported a huge jump in my platform visibility. It was in that moment I became clear that we are all better together.

SUPPORT IS ESSENTIAL

Since 2012, I have facilitated many webinars and tele-series. When I began, I had no idea how much time, energy and focus it would take to create a product of excellence. No success happens without a plan of execution and a way to carry it out.

I may be the "face" of the series, but it was impossible to do it without amazing "behind the scenes" supporters.

What I didn't know when I began was what I needed to be successful. Here are some of the things that needed attention – and my team and I learned some of these the hard way!

» Opt-in pages – How you get people to know about your product and sign up.

» Appropriate technology support – audio and visual (which company best suits your needs. No one company does it all.)

» Secure payment structure – Must be able to handle large numbers of people (you and your audience need to feel safe).

» Scheduling of guests – These are busy people and need clarity.

» Communication with guests – You only get one chance to create excellence in relationships – my guests come back because my team and I treat them well.

» Writing of curriculum – Engaging, clear and focused material is a must.

» Creation of downloads for participants – Your audience needs take-aways.

» Refund policies – If you don't have published policies, you are bound to run into challenges with customers.

The scope of this partial list hopefully gives you an awareness that trying to do this alone could bring overwhelm and even failure. You are not a one-person band. Get intentional about bringing on knowledgeable people who can assist you in constructing great product and credibility.

I knew I was going to need to invest, but I didn't have a lot of money to do my first online works. I believe that paying people for their work is important and creates trust, so I bartered for assistance. I did profit sharing. I carefully hired hourly people to support me in the most crucial times. These people helped me create an infrastructure that continues to grow and serve more people. Some of my original team members are still with me and some are not, but I am clear how our partnerships supported me in being where I am today.

Things continue to shift because technology is changing rapidly. However, the team I have today is committed, efficient and happy to grow with my organization. We are partners in collaboration.

MASTERMINDS ARE POWERFUL GIFTS

A mastermind group is a collaboration of people who brainstorm together and share experiences and ideas that can support the group to expand in different areas of their lives. There is powerful energy, growth, and excitement that participants bring to a mastermind. The fabulous thing is that participants challenge each other to create, identify and implement goals and new concepts. They support each through honesty, respect and compassion.

Several years ago, a man I barely knew contacted me. He was a very successful entrepreneur and corporate coach. He asked me to join a mastermind group with him and a few other people. I was perplexed. My business was small and I was still very active in ministry. I questioned his invitation, and he told me that he thought I would bring a different point of view and engagement. When I got to the table, every person did something different and there were multiple levels of experience and success. The members of the team supported me in thinking bigger and daring to step boldly forward. I gave them tools for emotional integration and spiritual acumen. It was a perfect marriage.

That group proved to be one of the most amazing experiences of my life. During the time of our being together, my business structure became anchored, my marketing materials solidified and my visibility platform went up 20%.

BUILDING PARTNERSHIP EXERCISES

• • • • •

BUILDING AFFILIATES AND JOINT VENTURES

You want to find people who are in alignment with your vision, honor your work in the world and want to be in collaboration to build both of your businesses. They will, and should, ask you to reciprocate when they have a program. So, make sure you believe in what they do. Here are ways to develop these partnerships:

» Reach out to people with whom you have established relationships and see if they are interested in being an affiliate.

» Follow people you admire on social media and enter dialogues with them to create relationships.

» Only invite people with whom you feel secure sharing with your list. Total strangers are generally risky and can alienate people you have nurtured.

OPT-IN PAGES

Every online event needs one of these. Here are the things you need to make it attractive to customers. This is a powerful way to build your mailing list once you have a product you believe in.

The headline: Catchy headlines capture attention immediately.

The benefits: What problem are you solving? Use simple language and bullet points.

The call to action: You have to ask them to sign up.

The opt-in form: This is the way they sign up and you capture their information.

HERE ARE QUESTIONS TO ASK YOURSELF WHEN GETTING READY TO CREATE AN OFFERING AND MARKET IT TO YOUR AUDIENCE:

What are you offering?

What problem are you solving?

What do you want them to do?

Why should they trust you?

How will you keep customers engaged?

Who will build your opt-in page?

Who will manage feedback with customers?

Who will support editing for curriculum?

Who will be your online support?

Who will support your social media?

Who will support your affiliates?

HERE ARE QUESTIONS TO ASK WHEN ARE VETTING AN AFFILIATE OR JOINT VENTURE PARTNER:

What is their "why?"

What do they value?

Are their values in alignment with yours?

How do they treat their customers?

What experience do you have with them in business?

Are you willing to share this company/person with your list?

Do they have a good track record of integrity doing business?

VISIONING/MEDITATION QUESTIONS

If you have not participated in visioning before, you want to understand that this is not mediation. This is a process to tap into the universe and ask powerful questions. I like to ask my heart to

participate in the process. Take your time and understand that there is no "one way" to do this. The answers that come are right.

Find a time to get still. You want this to be a time when you will not be interrupted. Have a journal or paper close to you so that you can write down what comes to you in this process. You might feel energy, see colors and images, or hear words or phrases. Some people just have a sense of peace or love. Remember, there is no perfect way to do this. Just contemplate each question and write down what comes to you. You will not lose your connection when you write. You just write and close your eyes again. A field of unconditional love is the place where you start.

Sit back and allow your body to sink into your seat. Be reminded that you are fully supported. Gently close your eyelids and begin to breathe. There is no effort required; just breathe and allow the breath to move up your feet to your legs. Let the breath continue up your thighs and around your hips. Now, let it go up your spine and wrap around your stomach. Breathe in and let the breath move into your chest and around your neck. Let it fill your head. Continue to breathe until you can feel your body relax.

Imagine that you are surrounded by unconditional love, and it is bathing you. Your relaxation becomes deeper. It is from this place that you will contemplate the following questions:

What is the highest vision for partners in my business?

What must I become to attract these partners?

What must I release?

What must I receive and embrace?

Is there anything else I need to know in this moment?

Now, reconnect to the breath and the body. Slowly bring your attention back to your room and open your eyes. Write any last-minute things that might have come through.

Do this process several times and you will begin to see themes. You will also begin to experience synchronicities in people you meet or who are attracted to your brand.

LIFE LESSONS TO LIVE BY WHEN YOU HAVE BEEN LAID OFF

* * * * *

—Lynda King

After working for 25 years, can you imagine losing two jobs in 90 days? Yep, that is what happened, and I can honestly say it was the best thing I could have experienced.

At the time, I didn't understand that I was being prepared for the event, but it is crystal clear now.

Being a master worrier does have its advantages. I actually melted down with my first full-blown anxiety attack three months prior to being laid off. This was useful because, when the actual event happened, I had already experienced firsthand how unproductive the anxiety attack was so I didn't have to experience another one.

At an event I attended, the speaker asked a question: "Would it be all right if life got a little bit easier?" At the time, I was almost insulted at how simple that statement was, but was intrigued to learn more. It just so happened that, now that I no longer had a job, I had the time to attend the workshop called "Mastering Life's Energy." In that course, I was introduced to the concepts about attracting an abundance of resources: time, love, money and joy to my life with the new understanding that one without the others was not going to allow me to create the life I knew I deserved.

I was also blessed to meet a few people who would become lifelong friends and mentors. I knew Tom was one of the first calls I needed to make. The call started, "Hi, this is Lynda King, not sure you remember me?"

His response was a resounding: "Remember you? You were the angel who walked into my life with answers to key questions when I was searching for my life purpose. Of course I remember you." In this important conversation, Tom set me straight on how to approach finding my next opportunity. In fact, he was very clear that I actually should not be relying on myself to find the job but turn it over to the Universe and let my next opportunity find me. Tom said to me, "I am sure you have an amazing imagination, but why would you limit your possibilities to what you can imagine when you have experienced things like the Grand Canyon?" At that moment, I decided I will do this a new way.

I had to establish a healthy relationship with time. I would have to be accountable to new choices in every area.

The next step was to develop a new relationship with money. In my first conversation with my financial planner, he was asked the obvious question: "how much did you make and what are your monthly expenses?" At first I did not think he believed me when I said, "I honestly don't know." In our next conversation, I shared with him that I was not going to count the pennies; I wanted to count the moments (at this point I think he might have thought I was delirious...when in fact, I was completely serious). I had figured out that if I lived until I was 90 and slept 7 hours per day, I had about 11 million moments left. I wanted to spend them well, creating memories along the way.

As it turns out, I was off work for 42 of 52 weeks that year and I took the opportunity to spend those moments wisely. I shifted my core belief systems in three key ways:

> » **I shifted to the concept that life could be easy.** In fact, I went to Staples and bought several "easy" buttons so I could remind myself.
>
> » **I shifted my thinking to *what can I say yes to*?** Sure enough, an invitation came for me to trek in the Himalayas the same day my second job was eliminated. As I thought through the decision

process between house payments and the trip to India, I knew I would always have house payments, but would not ever have a chance to celebrate my friend's 50th birthday in the Himalayas again... the decision was obvious to me: I have to say yes to the trip to the Himalayas. For most people in my life, that was almost crazy, as I had never hiked or camped in my life. I knew I needed to be taken far outside my comfort zone, as that is where the important lessons are learned.

» **I had to shift my belief system about being taken care of and thinking that I was responsible for everything**...and then I experienced a miracle that shifted that belief system. I got a call on a Saturday morning from someone who said they had found my daughter's checkbook. I was somewhat concerned, as she had traveled out of town that morning. When I got off the phone, I checked her account online and didn't see any unusual transactions. I had the address where I was supposed to pick up the checkbook. Being cautious, I asked my husband to drive me there. As we drove to the location, I remembered the name on the caller ID was familiar to me. When I spoke to the person who answered the door, I asked, "Did your Dad work at ACI? Was his name Bob?" Both answers were yes. I called Bob, who I had worked with for many years, and asked where he'd found the checkbook. He was driving down Maple Street at 50 miles per hour and he saw the checkbook on the side of the road and stopped to pick it up. Really, who notices things on the side of the road driving 50 mph? At that moment I knew, if God could take care of something as detailed as keeping my daughter's checkbook safe, I didn't have to worry anymore, because God would take care of me always.

The rest of my time off was filled with miracles and supportive partnerships that I could never have imagined. I learned to ask for help and trust that I would be fully supported.

YOUR INNER LIFE

This section focuses on keeping you balanced. We cannot be our most powerful person without the ability to stay centered. Use this information to anchor your choices to create peace and harmony in your life.

CHAPTER ELEVEN

Spiritual Growth

• • • • •

Since the only life you can have is the life of the Spirit within you, you need but permit Its radiance to flow through your thoughts into self-expression. You are surrounded by a dynamic force, a great surge of living power. You are immersed in and saturated with the vital essence of Life. Its presence permeates everything, binding all together in one complete whole.

—Ernest Holmes

This chapter is NOT about religion. I am very clear that there is not one path to peace and enlightenment. We are all spiritual beings, having an experience in human form. I truly believe that we are here to learn lessons in caring, love, compassion and service. Sometimes it is easy and sometimes it is hard; there is no getting around it. Whatever the experience, we all have a strong spiritual essence at the core of our being. Our job is to remember and connect to that powerful universal center.

When you hold a newborn, you know that what I am saying is true. There is sweetness and a peace that is profound in nature. Your only response can be to feel the love and give it back to the being you hold. Babies are reminders that we came on this planet as reflections of pure love. Somehow, we forget.

I grew up in the African Methodist Episcopal church and I was surrounded by a group of deeply religious women. They were also spiritual in profound ways. The women in my family were prophetic dreamers. Meaning, they saw the future through dreams. No one talked about it except when someone would say, "I dreamed Mary was pregnant." The next week Mary would announce she was having a baby. Everyone would just smile and have no conversation about how amazing that was. I remember overhearing my mom talking to her sister about dreaming her fiancé was going to drown a few weeks before that happened. I was too scared to inquire too deeply, since it seemed like a secret.

I had those dreams too, but learned quickly not to tell anyone. As a young child, I thought this was normal and would tell my friends the dreams I had about them. The dreams would come true and gradually they began to call me a witch. That was a clear signal that everyone didn't have these experiences. I began to think that there was something wrong with my family and me. It was many years later that I put the pieces together and realized that I, like many others on the planet, was gifted with high intuition and the ability to "see" and understand things beyond the physical world. It wasn't just in dreams; I would have thoughts about something or someone, and they would occur. I would sit with people and have impressions come to my mind just before they shared exactly what I was thinking. I would start to journal, and messages would come through my writing that clearly were not my language or rhythm. These messages became the foundation for much of the work I do today.

The definition of intuition is the ability to understand something immediately, without the need for conscious reasoning. I had no idea that we all had intuitive natures and we could learn to expand them to use for our growth. No one in my family or circle of friends talked about the ability to connect to things beyond our education or knowledge base. People would ignore the fact that a mother knew her child was in danger before getting the news of an accident. Gifts of jobs or money would come in the "nick of time," and everyone would say it was time to be grateful. I kept wondering who or what we were being grateful to, and weren't *we* involved somehow? Our culture told us to only trust what we can see and to only put your faith in that which is tangible. So, when synchronicities would occur, I began to write it off as a coincidence. Also, with my religious upbringing, there were a lot of superstitions about the "dark side" long before Star Wars.

As I opened to realizing that my spiritual nature was vast and that the gifts I had been given were here to support my purpose, I began to explore. I took classes, workshops, and went on spiritual retreats. I learned that there was something called Ancient Wisdom and that, for centuries, people had practiced connecting to a higher power in extraordinary ways. I was elated. In each place of exploration, I kept hearing that when you are in your lowest place you can surrender to God and you will be guided - but surrender to anything or anyone felt scary. I wasn't even sure what that meant until my world fell apart.

I was in the middle of an unpleasant divorce. My acting career was crumbling. I was responsible for my children, mother and my grandmother's care. My brother was estranged from our family. My self-esteem was in the toilet and I was an emotional wreck. I couldn't think straight and everything I said seemed to be irrational and paranoid in nature. To say I was feeling lost is an understatement.

Everywhere I went, people were saying, "just surrender." That statement just enraged me and I withdrew. I wanted to lash out at everyone, and I was in a place of being a total victim. I spent my time watching soap operas and eating non-nourishing food. It felt like I was dying, except I wasn't. What *was* dying was my incessant ego chatter and the belief that I was in control of anything.

One day I was driving down the street and saw a billboard with my ex-husband's face. I screamed, "Why me?" Then, I heard a voice say, "Because you are to see the God in him." I slammed on the brakes and looked around. No one was there but me. I slowly drove forward and the voice said, "He is your great teacher." Now, some of you are probably thinking this is a little crazy. I don't blame you; so did I. I went to my therapist and told him that I was losing it and probably needed drugs. He said, "Maybe it is your subconscious giving you information." That turned out to be true in ways I could not have imagined.

YOUR PAST DOES NOT DEFINE YOU

The work with the therapist over the next few weeks was about my identity. I identified myself as a victim and it went all the way back to my early childhood. The abuse from my stepfather was only one place. At three years old, I got locked in a dark basement by my babysitter. I was told that the bogey man was going to get me. For many years, I had horrible dreams and was afraid to be in the dark.

One day while I was in a big meltdown, the therapist looked at me and said, "Your past does not define you." I looked at him in awe. What if that were true? What if my past was just a part of who I am? What if I was more than the trauma of my childhood?

It took many years of continued therapy and studying spiritual psychology and interpersonal development to get clear that everything that happened to me was a part of who I was, and that I could choose how I showed up in the world. I could choose to respond from a new perspective and identify myself as healthy, vibrant, safe and loved.

I am not saying to forget what happened: that is impossible. It did happen and, for some of us, the "it" was terrifying and horrible. It does not, however, have to be the way you walk through the world forever. It isn't always easy, but YOU do get to choose.

I am clear that what happened to me as a child and everything thereafter made me who I am today. It is a key component of the passion I feel in the work I do with others. Once I got clear that my pain could be transformed to passion, my life took off. I still have moments of the old fear coming in, but I now have the tools to choose differently. My life is a design of my making, and so is yours.

You are here for a reason. You are here to fully express. You are made of a divine substance. Quantum physicists call it the quantum field – an energy field made up of infinite possibilities. If this is true, then you can reach into that field within you and pick peace, love, joy, freedom, creativity and expansion. It is available in every moment.

Your body holds the key

There is a lot of talk about the mind/body connection. So, I want to invite you into this conversation. What if your body was like a computer and remembered everything that ever happened to you? What if it responded to life based on triggers of memory encoded in your DNA? Today, that is exactly what science is telling us. In fact, there is a great deal of study about historical trauma.

The body has its own language, and it is important to learn it. I believe it tells us when we are challenged before we are consciously aware that a problem exists.

Emotions are recycled energy. When we are healthy, they tell us how we feel and help us be aware of our thoughts and behaviors. When we are not healthy, our bodies begin to tell us that we are out of sync. The body begins to show us how we are thinking, acting and feeling, especially when we are stressed or anxious. Here are some of the ways it can show up:

» Headaches

» Overeating

» Weight gain or loss

» High blood pressure

» Constipation or diarrhea

» Dry mouth

» Extreme tiredness

» Trouble sleeping

» Lightheadedness

» Racing heart

» Sexual problems

» Shortness of breath

» Back pain

» Stiff neck

» Hormonal imbalance

These symptoms can be related to other things, but it is important to recognize that the mind and the body do connect. In the work I do with clients, called Emotional Integration, we look at the body first. As they are sharing an experience, I invite them to connect to the part of the body that feels the most constricted in that moment. Many times it is in the heart, throat, stomach or lower back. In the exploration we often discover unremembered childhood challenges or traumas. They recall information about fight or flight responses that were created to escape violent experiences or emotional conditioning.

Once the memory comes to the surface, we can do things to reframe the non-supportive decisions that were made and have been running their entire lives. This is done through movement, creative exercises, integration techniques, affirmations, meditations, journaling and prayer from any path they choose. I am clear that we can use spiritual tools to reclaim the pure nature that lives within us all.

SPIRITUAL PRACTICE AS A TOOL

There is no one spiritual practice that works for everyone. Some people love to meditate and others cannot shut down the monkey mind that chatters incessantly. There is a great deal of evidence that meditation supports the mental and physical body. It can support the immune system, the lowering of blood pressure and stress management. Some use affirmations - words that affirm a truth we want to embody - to bring them back to center. Others are clear that prayer, in any form, is the thing that reminds them that they are cared for no matter the experience that is unfolding.

For me, I use many spiritual tools daily, and have done so for over 30 years. Not every tool works in every moment. I remember feeling like I had lost my connection to Spirit, and the only thing that would calm me down was listening to quiet music and looking at a video of crystals changing form. Somehow, I could get lost in the images and the music. That process supported me in finding my way back to a deeper practice.

I have an active personality. So, in the beginning, sitting down and meditating was a challenge. I began doing five minutes a day. Since I had a Christian upbringing, I used a statement from the Bible: "The Lord is my shepherd." Anytime my mind would wander, I would say that phrase. It was excruciating. Time seemed to move slowly, and I kept looking at my watch. When that would happen, I would take a breath and say the phrase. Today, my spiritual practice is 45 minutes to an hour. I meditate for 30-45 minutes, read something inspirational, journal and then set my intentions for the day. I no longer need a mantra. I can almost always depend on my breath to take me to center.

Whatever you choose, do something every day. Repeat an affirmation for peace. "I live a life that is filled with peace and love." It can be that simple. Just start. Get a book on meditation or affirmations. I have meditation CDs, and so do many other teachers, coaches and healers. Keep looking until you find something that works for you. Once you begin to practice, you will find that each day is less stressful and that you are responding differently to life.

SPIRITUAL PRACTICE EXERCISES

. . . . .

AFFIRMATIONS (USE ONE OR MORE DAILY):

Today, I stand in the awareness that I am powerful, beautiful and gifted.

I am fully equipped to handle anything today.

Today, I bring my best self to my work and to my life.

I radiate joy and peace wherever I am.

I am healthy in mind, body and spirit.

I am destined for success and I claim it now.

Love expresses through me in every relationship.

Money is my friend and I am open to receiving extraordinary wealth.

SHORT READINGS

Future

Mahatma Gandhi tells us that our beliefs, thoughts, words, actions, habits and values create our destiny. That means that our future is up to us. We have the power to create a life that is filled with harmony, peace and prosperity. All that is required is a willingness to take one step at a time into a marvelous future of infinite possibilities. Each step can be overflowing with the promise of a life that is filled with creativity, poise and expansion. The future does not exist until we step into it as a "power-filled present." Today, build your future by monitoring your beliefs, thoughts, words, actions, habits and values. If you do this from a place of unlimited possibility, you must step into a future that is limitless.

Today, I call forth my amazing future and leap into it with great expectancy of good.

Trust

We have all heard the statement "just trust." The challenge is to trust when your world, your relationship, your job or your finances seem to be falling apart. This is the time that we are called to remember that change is inevitable and may not be comfortable. We are called to let go of the old and open to the new. In the midst of that discomfort there is the divine opportunity to activate a trust that you are supported. It is the time to remember that you are centered in the infinite energy of grace, and it is guiding you always. Trust is being willing to let go and be open to what is next for you. Trust is an aspect of faith that requires each of us to allow the perfection of Spirit to be revealed in the midst of any effect.

Today, I activate trust that I am fully supported and deeply loved.

Truth

It is said that it is the truth that sets us free. Not a truth based on concepts that are judgment-filled, but a truth that is anchored in the reality of unity. To tell the Truth means to be absolutely sure that the presence of the Spirit is everywhere. It is your life. It is the life of every man, woman and child. It is the Truth of every religion, every lifestyle and culture. This Truth is undeniable. This Truth is a golden thread that connects us all.

Today, I speak my truth with love and authenticity. I connect to the oneness that exists within us all.

Receptivity

For many of us, it is easier to give than to receive. It is easier to extend our selves than to accept random acts of kindness. Wouldn't it be wonderful if we really stood in a place of understanding that the flow of the universe includes receiving? What if today we all stopped and recognized the beauty of receiving? We could then let go of old statements like, "It is more blessed to give than to receive." We could open our hearts and allow the energy of unconditional love to act as a bridge to receptivity. We could bring to our conscious an awareness that the act of receiving is also supporting someone else to live a life of fulfillment and sharing.

Today, I activate the law of circulation. I give and receive with great enthusiasm.

Struggle

There is a belief in our culture that struggle is inevitable. In fact, many of us were brought up in environments where we were told that we had to struggle to be successful. My question is, "Why would a God of love create a life that needed to struggle?" That feels like a misguided concept. We came here to be joyous, expansive, enthusiastic and powerful. There is no need to struggle. Grace is everywhere and is available now. We can open to an ease in living; all that is needed is to open up and say, "Yes!" The Universe will do the rest.

Today, I am a total yes for ease and grace to fill my life and my choices.

Love

Love lives within us all. That is why we crave it so desperately. Every person on this planet wants to feel love, experience love and express love. If that is true, love must be a healing salve that we are called to apply in every area of our lives. It must be our responsibility to bring love into existence in the physical world. It must be our responsibility to start with a love of self and then radiate out into the world. If everyone did that, there would be no need for hate, war or separation.

Today, I consciously shine the light of love that lives within me and share it with everyone I meet. I see the love that lives within each person.

I AM MEDITATION

Put on some peaceful music before you begin the meditation...

Begin with the breath and gently center yourself. Allow each breath to fill you with light. Begin to feel the relaxation and be totally present in the room. Breathe in love and breathe out peace. Now activate your imagination. If you are visual, you will see things. If not, just feel into the experience. As you listen to the music, slowly move to a beautiful sanctuary. This is a safe, beautiful place that nurtures and comforts you. Take a few moments to be still and witness the beauty of your sanctuary.

Invite in a guide (animal, person, angel, or just energy). Feel the love coming from the guide. Ask the guide its name. The guide will be with you for the rest of the journey. Begin to explore your sanctuary. You may find new paths, new doorways, and new rooms. Notice the feeling tones in your body as you explore.

Soon you see a beautiful tall mirror standing alone. Walk to the mirror and when you look in, you see the reflection of how THE UNIVERSE SEES YOU. Witness the beauty and magnificence. Look in the mirror and say, "I AM." The reflection will say words back to you. Now pick a word to repeat each time (love, peace, joy, abundant, free, expansive, held, honored, seen—or use your own) "I AM"....... "I AM"....... "I AM"....... "I AM"....... (take in the words) "I AM"....... "I AM"....... "I AM".......

Do this until you feel peaceful and calm. Now, gently move away from the mirror and walk with your guide to a beautiful pool filled with warm water. Gently remove your clothing and get into the water. This is a healing pool. As you sit with the guide, share any areas of your life that you have a hard time seeing yourself as the universe sees you. The guide will simply listen. You begin to hear voices in the distance. It is a chant. Close your eyes and allow the warm water to soothe you as the chant comes closer. The pool is surrounded by angels singing the chant about the truth of who you are. "YOU ARE"... "YOU ARE"... "YOU ARE"... "YOU ARE"... "YOU ARE"... Listen to all of the amazing things they are saying about you. Breathe it in.

The guide gently fades away and you slowly get out of the water. There are new clothes laying there for you. What color are they? What do the garments look like? Put on the new garments. Thank your guide. The guide tells you that you are loved and that they are here for you always. Gently leave your sanctuary and slowly, gently return to this space.

Journal for five minutes.

THE POWER OF SURRENDER AND RELEASE

* * * * *

—*Kellie Christina Jones*

For over 35 years my mother and I have had challenges communicating and understanding each other. My mother struggled with emotional and mental issues, which manifested as delusions and paranoia. As a child, I knew something was wrong, but no one would answer my questions. As my mother aged, the challenges escalated between us. I come from a family that does not believe in mental or emotional support from doctors or counselors. So, my mother has not been to a medical doctor in over 10 years.

One morning in March, 2015 at 5:00 a.m., I received a call from my mother. She was very disturbed and irrational. This had happened before, but something was particularly unnerving this time. Her paranoia was at an all-time high. She stated she was going to move in with my husband and me, and was not taking "no" for an answer. She was calling a cab to come to our home, and wanted to make sure I was there. However, we had moved from the place she thought she was going to four months earlier. She was filled with fury and rage when I reminded her that I no longer lived at that previous address. I felt her anger penetrating the phone line, and I had to get off the phone. I hung up and dropped to the floor. I felt afraid, helpless and powerless. I called my supportive husband. In his work in law enforcement, he specializes in working with people who have mental issues. I just cried and asked for help and prayer. I finally calmed down and stepped outside.

A gentle voice inside me said, "What do you want? Help is here, just ask."

I felt an energy shift in my body. I opened up my arms as wide as I could. I stated out loud to all of nature and universal source: "I quit, I give up! My mother is your child and I give her to you. Please help me. Thank you." A gust of wind moved through the yard. I literally felt a physical weight being removed from my body. I experienced ethereal arms around me. It was as if the clouds from the sky and tree branches were lovingly hugging and holding me in pure love and light.

The universe moves quickly when you engage the power of surrender and release. In less than 24 hours, I received a phone call from the hospital telling me that my mother had suffered a small fall. She did not break anything, but it was enough to get her proper care. The hospital performed many tests based on her age and outward behavior. The test results revealed challenges regarding both her physical and mental health. Some of the things I was aware of, and other challenges I learned had existed even prior to my birth.

The puzzle of my childhood experiences with regard to my mother were put into perspective in less than a week. She now had the proper care and support she needs and deserves, and my family and I are more at peace knowing she is receiving the help.

* * *

There is and undefinable power in utilizing the principles of surrender and release. This God-given power is within you and me, waiting to be birthed and to move into and throughout our lives on all levels. Surrendering and releasing is not giving up, falling down or quitting: it is a place of movement, rising up, clarity, choice and *power*. This power can assist you in changing circumstances in your life. This power changed and healed me, and I know it can do the same for you.

Now is the time to claim the power that lives within you. You are not experiencing the current circumstances alone. You can tap into the power of surrender and release. Meditation, prayer and other spiritual practice modalities can assist and support you letting go.

A beautiful song dropped into my being during one of my spiritual practices.

Feel free to use this mantra/song to help support you.

I Release, I Release!

I Let Go, I Let Go!

I now let the Divine to Flow!

Surrendering is a great evolutionary awakening for us all. Take a stand today.

CHAPTER TWELVE

EMOTIONAL WELL-BEING

• • • • •

Women in particular need to keep an eye on their physical and mental health, because if we're scurrying to and from appointments and errands, we don't have a lot of time to take care of ourselves. We need to do a better job of putting ourselves higher on our own "to do" list.

—Michelle Obama

But pain's like water. It finds a way to push through any seal. There's no way to stop it. Sometimes you have to let yourself sink inside of it before you can learn how to swim to the surface.

—Katie Kacvinsky

It has taken me a long time to understand the difference between responding and reacting. That is primarily because I have always been an emotional, highly sensitive being. I feel everything. I remember walking into rooms as a child and crying for no reason. Then I would learn there had been a death or someone had lost a job. I didn't understand why this happened. My family told me I was a cry-baby and not to be so emotional. The more I tried to listen to that advice, the more emotional I became. I tried not to cry: I tried to hide my feelings. I tried to disappear so that no one would know what I was feeling. None of that worked. I cried at home. I even cried at school, which made me a target for bullies.

All of the responses to my emotional outbursts coupled with my violent childhood filled me with rage, and I had frequent episodes of lashing out. When I was in the 6th grade, a boy named Arthur liked me. He was tall, lanky, very odd-looking, and his energy felt creepy to me. I tried to stay far away from him. One day, he cornered me in the coat closet and tried to kiss me. He had humongous lips and all I could see was those lips heading for my face. I went ballistic, leapt at him and tried to push him out of the window. The teacher burst in and screamed for me to stop. Arthur yelled, "You are crazy!" and I screamed, "And you are slimy!" Needless to say, that ended his crush and put me on the list of kids that act out.

I didn't know at that point that my response was over the top; I just felt this need to protect myself and fight for my rights. On one hand, I was fearless. On the other, I was terrified a lot of the time, and had no concept or understanding that I was taking on others' feelings. No one talked at that time about people having empathic abilities.

The definition of an empathic person is someone with the paranormal ability to apprehend the mental or emotional state of another individual. Here are some of the traits they exhibit:

» Knowing things without anyone telling them

» Being with a lot of people can feel overwhelming

» Taking on others' feelings as their own

» Watching horror movies or tragedies on television can be unbearable

» Having big BS detectors and knowing when people are being dishonest

» Feeling constant fatigue after being with people

» Developing addictive personalities to avoid feeling

» Experiencing intolerance of deceitful people

I had all of these traits, and I was constantly in trouble for my behavior. I knew when people were lying to others or me, and it was almost impossible to keep it to myself. I would have huge outbursts of anger when people didn't believe me, especially when I was telling them things I "knew" were true. When my predictions would come to pass, there was no acknowledgment of my gift. I began to distrust my feelings and my intuition. It was not uncommon for me to shut down, withdraw or lash out.

When I began to do emotional healing work and develop my integration processes, I used my own life experiences as a guideline.

YOUR HISTORY IS JUST A BLUEPRINT

A **blueprint** is a guide for making something—it's a design or pattern that can be followed. It is also a design that can be changed. While I was an associate minister at Mile Hi Church in Denver, we built a new sanctuary. The drawings were in and our Senior Minister, Dr. Roger Teel, had a profound meditation experience. He came back to the team and said, "We have to change the blueprint. This building needs to be a dome." He was so centered and so clear, we all knew it was the right thing to do.

What we discovered was that Monolithic Domes are proven survivors of tornadoes, hurricanes, earthquakes and fires. Dr. Teel's guidance allowed us to build a beautiful structure that was more safe and supportive for the community than the original design.

Your history is just a blueprint. It contains all of your experiences, life challenges and victories. However, the trajectory of your life can change by your intentionality, inner guidance and deep desire to step into your greatness. Every time you grow or experience a powerful revelation, you are affecting the grand design of your destiny. You are creating a new reality.

Consider the fact that Maya Angelou and Oprah Winfrey did not allow their historical blueprints to define their lives. Instead, they each chose to create a life that has inspired millions of people on this planet.

WHO'S IN CHARGE?

You can blame your parents and your past for only so long. Sooner or later, you have to take responsibility for your life and your choices. You are not a victim of life. You get to boldly step into your future and do fantastic things. No one else can deliver your message or the gifts you bring the way you can.

Freedom is available in every moment. I love Howard Thurman's writing. One of my favorite quotes on freedom is, "Often, to be free means the ability to deal with the realities of one's own situation so as not to be overcome by them."

No matter how much work you have done, how many workshops you have attended or how many years of therapy you have experienced, you are still human. You will have moments of doubt, fear, discomfort, anxiety and distrust. Here is my response to that statement: so what? So what if you falter? So what if you lose your temper and act inappropriately in any given moment? So what if someone annoys you? It is only a moment in time. You are in charge and, if something isn't working, you get to change it. You get to become clearer about your triggers and responses.

I learned many things when I attended the University of Santa Monica to study spiritual psychology, but one particular statement I learned there always comes to mind when I am challenged. The statement is: "How you deal with the issue is the issue." You get to decide what you will do next. No one can do it for you. No one can take your power. **You** give it away.

I believe we must become clear about the emotions that spiral us into deep holes of depression and immobility. One of the things I work with in client sessions is the understanding that there are younger parts of ourselves that have unresolved issues. Some people call this inner child work. I actually believe that these are parts of us that we have hidden away or pushed down because it was too painful to stay connected. Once we become aware of them, they become great allies of transformation. In fact, I think these parts act out to get our attention and ask for our awakening.

YOUR BEHAVIOR AND EMOTIONS ARE LINKED

Have you ever thought about unresolved rage? Most of us don't want to get angry or deal with angry people. I cannot tell you how many clients have told me, "I don't get angry." That is interesting to me, because these are people who have been abused, traumatized, betrayed and mistreated. How can you not be angry about that stuff on some level?

When we finally get to a place of safety, we can often see how the pain was so intense that the only response was to run from it. That can look like overeating, drugs and alcohol, becoming a workaholic or consistently attracting dramatic experiences.

When we experience rage, we each react differently. Some of us become angry. Some of us do bizarre and inappropriate things. Some of us become super sweet and deny feelings.

What do you think could be the out-picturing of unresolved rage?

Here's a partial list of what it could look like:

Relationship challenges

Body challenges

Job challenges

Financial challenges

Inappropriate behavior

Clinical depression

Isolation

Self-sabotage

Violence

Addiction

Memory loss

Self-condemnation

Inability to hear higher self

Lack of spontaneity

Low self-esteem

You cannot hide, pray away, journal away or run from your rage—because it will leap out when you least expect it. You must become clear about your relationship to rage and how it blocks your expansion.

Rage and anger are not your enemies: they are here to assist you in taking control of your life. They are here to help you heal and express powerfully. It's important that you get clear about what pain you are running from and face it. The thing we don't understand is that we must honor the rage, embrace it and love it. Our goal should be to transform pain to its highest vibrational state. If you do not, you will continue to choose stuff that is not good for you. The pain is here to help you heal. It is an energetic magnet that keeps bringing experiences to you to assist in shifting old decisions and beliefs. Denial prolongs the discomfort. You must get it out, or it will never let go of you. It will continue to show up in people and circumstances until you are willing to do things differently. You must identify it to change it. When you get clear about what you're feeling—the anger, the rage—then you can begin to shift it.

By the way, people can see and feel that you are angry, upset or wearing a mask. Energy can be and is felt, even if you don't say a word. You cannot hide your energy, whether or not you speak it. You must do something to get this energy out of your body—otherwise it will show up in ways you don't want.

You want to get to a place where you understand that the soul's desire is for love to be present. The pain is a gateway to your freedom.

EMOTIONAL INTEGRATION EXERCISE

• • • • •

QUESTIONS FOR CHANGE

Here are some tools for identifying unresolved rage and shifting your relationship to that rage. When you are upset, pause and ask yourself the following questions:

What does it feel like when I'm angry, when I'm in rage, when I'm upset? Does my body get tense? What else?

How do I respond to it? Do I withdraw my energy? Do I lash out? Do I cry? Do I scream?

What happens in my body? Does my throat become constricted? My heart? My solar plexus?

Do I lose sleep? Do my shoulders tighten, my neck? Do I shut down sexually?

What is my internal decision? "I can't win this fight, so I'll just shut down." "I'll become a warrior and slash anyone in my way." "I'll stuff this feeling because it's too scary to let out." "I will anchor more inwardly so that my voice is not important and I can't make a difference, so I won't try."

What is my external behavior? Do I pretend that it doesn't matter? Do I move into a state of victimhood? Do I sabotage myself by doing things that don't support me and push people away?

Does what I'm doing support peace—internally or externally?

The moment you can wake up and answer these questions, you will begin to become aware of how you can move out of your pain. The answers might not come easily because you are conditioned to turn your back on feeling, but I promise if you do this exercise consistently, change will come.

AFFIRMATIONS:

My feelings are here to support my health and well-being. I embrace them and make choices that honor my life.

I am strong enough in any moment to see, honor and embrace any feeling. I choose how I will respond in every moment.

I am powerful and see my past as a gift. My future is in my hands. I give thanks for every emotion. I am alive and I can feel. What a gift.

TIME TO PLAY:

Create a list of things that you LOVE to do. Things that make you feel happy, joyous, young at heart and playful. Now, put one thing a week from this list on your calendar. Make it a non-negotiable calendar event. Do this for 30 days and see how much lighter you feel. I guarantee you that putting play on your schedule will remind you of the joy that children so naturally exhibit. (By the way, this is only 4 times in a month. I know you can do it.)

LEARNING TO PUT ME FIRST

• • • • •

—Lynne Snyder

I'm sitting in my son's house in Burbank, California feeling a bit sorry for myself after spending the last two days taking care of my two grandsons. Don't get me wrong, I love my grandsons, but my son is back in Colorado visiting with my two daughters (his sisters) and attending his friend's wedding, while I'm here supervising the care of his boys because his ex-wife is an unreliable caretaker.

This pity party has been going on for a few months now. My head keeps getting stuck in this constant thought pattern of: "I'm always there for my kids and grandkids, why don't they see that?" "How come they don't choose to come see me?" "They go visit their father, and he never helps them like I do."

That all sounds pretty sad, doesn't it? It's not like I expect them to gush all over me all the time; at least I don't think so. I just feel a little left out. My ex-husband got a cabin for this coming Christmas and invited all of them to stay with him there. He has never done anything like that and has rarely come to visit them, especially when they were growing up. My son will probably come back to Colorado then, but it will be to see his father.

My upset deepens. I'm always doing things for them like babysitting or even sending money, and yet I don't feel like they spend very much time making an effort to be with me. Even my grandkids have gotten used to having me around, and I feel like I'm not that "special" to them because I'm always there. I guess it all hurts my feelings a little.

Finally, I stop and realize this has been a pattern all of my life. I "sacrifice" my time, my money, my whatever so others, especially my children or partners, can have fun or be happy. Then I sit around and feel sorry for myself because I'm feeling left out.

This seems to be a little bit of a theme at work, as well. So, I'm sitting here in this hot apartment, waiting for my son's ex-wife to call me to come get the boys. I realize this all sounds pretty pathetic!

Then the revelation comes: I have wasted a lot of years giving my time, my money and physical energy away to others. I realize I don't need to sacrifice my life to love them. They haven't really asked me to give myself away. I can't imagine any of them turning their back on me if I started doing things for myself. I have enough love for them and me, and will probably have more energy if I start loving myself first.

I realized, too, that I have been kind of numb to my feelings and emotions for several years. I had to put my precious cat to sleep six weeks ago, and I realized my heart was breaking in two. For the first time in a long time I was having really deep feelings. I think that woke me up! There is a place for me in the world. It is time for me to step up and claim that place, which means creating life on my own terms.

I know that in the past I've insisted that I can't do the things I want to do like quit my job, be a counselor/coach, change my relationship, or just live because of no real reasons other than a blanket fear. I put into motion things that should give me the freedom to allow me to do anything I choose, and yet I don't take action to follow my proclaimed dreams. Then I wonder, "Do I really know what I want at all? Why?" Because I've been repeating the same stories over and over and telling myself I can't move or change.

I think I've been waiting for permission. From who and for what? I don't know. Anyone. God. Spirit. The Universe. I have been waiting on permission to soar, to succeed and find my real purpose. My purpose, which I know is to help raise the consciousness of the Universe, can't be done by me playing small anymore. It can't be done by me taking care of everyone else's needs.

I am choosing to change. I am now going to maneuver through any shame, guilt and fear. This first means I am living life the way I want to—not the way others expect me to. I have a vision of the world and my place in it. It looks like me being in joy, and showing others how to find that joy in their life, too. I know this will not be easy, as I have created strong patterns in my life, so I just need to take one day at a time. Recognizing that I need to put me first is the beginning.

CHAPTER THIRTEEN

CREATING SACRED SPACE

• • • • •

The calm within the storm is where peace lives and breathes. It is not within perfect circumstances or a charmed life...it is not conditional. Peace is a sacred space within, it is the temple of our internal landscape. We are free to visit it, whenever we seek sanctuary. Underneath the chaos of everyday living, peace is patiently awaiting our discovery...go within.

—Jaeda DeWalt

Create a sacred space to learn more about your body and mind, go on a date with yourself and explore emotions, sensation, desires, dreams, and accept yourself as you are. By spending some time getting to know yourself better, you will know what you have to offer and it will be easier to ask for what you want.

—Nityananda Dasa

I take people on pilgrimages to sacred sites around the world. We have walked the labyrinth in the Chartres Cathedral in France, been to Machu Picchu in Peru, traveled the path of Mary Magdalene in the South of France and meditated in the Temples of Humankind in Italy. A sacred space is any space or area that has been devoted to the purpose of something sacred. It can be found in places designated by world religions (temples, churches, synagogues, mosques), OR it can be at home—an office, a studio or your body. The important thing about a sacred space is the energy and intentionality that is put into it.

I saw a client recently who had been given abrupt notice to move and find a new home. There were mixed emotions. There was an attachment to the current space, but the new place that had been rented was open, light-filled and expansive. It was smaller, so she was releasing and throwing out many things, including items in a storage unit. We talked about how so many people in America have multiple storage units that they never visit. My mind jumped to the reality show about people bidding on storage spaces in case there was something valuable in them. I asked what was the intention for the new space. She said, "I want it to be more than an act of simplification. I want it to be a whole new beginning."

I have felt that way many times when I moved, wanting the space to feel new and clean. Here is the thing: we take ourselves with us everywhere we go. A space can only be what we make it by placing our energy and light there. It is actually not about the space itself - it is about the love, care and rituals that will live there that make it sacred.

I have never left a home without doing a thanksgiving and gratitude blessing for the space – even if there have been challenges that pushed me to the edge. That place was where my soul agreed to grow, and my honoring of that truth always allowed me to leave feeling clean.

I also bless each new home or office. I call in high vibrational energy and set an intention for the space to be loving and joyous.

YOU ARE A SANCTUARY

Periodically, there are uproars in the media or on social media about a woman being too risqué because she showed off her body in a way that society did not think was appropriate. Some of the women were scantily clothed. Others were full-sized. I am not an advocate for dishonoring the feminine form, but I am here to say that we women must come to terms with the fact that the body we inhabit is a sacred vessel. It is our job to celebrate it, love it, express in it and be unafraid to honor it.

One of my art expressions is the way that I dress. I am meticulous about what I put on my body and how I leave my house. I want to feel good, look good and share my love of beauty through my attire. I am bold, creative and oftentimes unexpected in the ways I dress. It took me a long time to get to this place because, quite frankly, I didn't want to be seen. Being visible in my childhood meant becoming a target for violence or sexual abuse. I did not feel safe in my body. My daughter-in-law used to say to me, "Mom, why don't you show your body?" She was referring to the fact that I only ever wore goddess attire. It was lovely, but you had to have a great imagination to ascertain what was underneath the draping. Today, I am much more comfortable and wear clothes that show off my figure.

Let me back up here for a moment. One of the other reasons I covered my body was that I was overweight. The stress of my life activated the behavior of "stress eating." Plus, my plate was so full that I wasn't working out. That proved to be a lethal combination that put 30 extra pounds on my body. I knew I wasn't taking care of myself and it showed. So, I just hid it.

One day, I had the thought: If my body is my temple, I am not doing a good job of taking care of it. I made of list of what it takes to honor a temple or sacred space:

1. Beautiful art and environment

2. Clear of clutter and clean

3. Plenty of stillness and silence (rest)

4. Respecting the space

Those four things became the foundation for putting attention on loving my body, my environment and me. I redid my office. I cleaned out my closets and released paper. I changed my diet, starting with a cleanse. I joined a gym and got a trainer. I became consistent in getting massages at least once a month. I was aware this was all external stuff, but I had to start somewhere. The next steps were to clear out my consciousness.

DE-CLUTTER FROM THE INSIDE OUT

If you want to know how you are living, look at your environment. Are you hoarding, cluttered, or rigid in your care of the space? I have been in people's homes that are beautiful, and it is made clear that you are not to touch anything. Those people are also operating in a world where they control everything in their life space.

My mother created her safety by surrounding herself with stuff. At one point, my brother and I spent days clearing out boxes, books and clothes to create a beautiful space. It was spectacular. Within a few months, she had asked for it all to come back. She "needed" this one thing. It was at that point that I realized that we could clear the clutter in her house, but not in her mind. The clutter represented how she felt in her life.

Here are some ways to know you need support on an internal level:

1. Stressed out and feeling uncomfortable, discontent, angry and withdrawn.

2. Consumed thinking, analyzing or trying to understand someone else's behavior.

3. Binge eating to find comfort.

4. Restless and having a hard time sleeping.

5. Working 12-16 hours a day.

6. No time for friends and family connection.

7. Obligated to put others before you and then feeling resentful.

8. Finding yourself barking at people and then feeling bad.

9. Constantly sick and fatigued.

10. Body is breaking down and you feel helpless to do anything about it.

11. Can't easily find anything in your office.

12. Closets and drawers are jammed full.

Any or all of these indicators are telling you to pause, take stock and do something different. You cannot make clear decisions if you are running in circles and your body is run down. This is not the time to do more or try to figure it out. You cannot create a solution from the level that the problem exists. If you feel confused and exhausted, your decision-making ability is diminished and cloudy. You want to get support, find a way to rest, and take inventory of what is really necessary in your life.

The same principles for decluttering space apply to your emotional levels.

» Make a list of what you want to achieve (get clear about your need to clear).

» Write down the beliefs and habits that keep you feeling stuck (look honestly at your space and see what is not working).

» Let go of anything that no longer serves you (throw it away or give it away if you haven't used it in six months or more).

» Find new containers (structures) to support you (put things where you can find them—boxes or containers).

» Designate quiet time to get clear (evaluate how you feel when you purge and feel organized).

YOUR PERSONAL ALTAR

I love this process because it is so personal. I have seen altars in homes, offices and throughout buildings in spiritual centers. There are no hard and fast rules. You just want to make sure that it is meaningful for you. Before you create it, set an intention and build it from that space. You will find that once the intention is set, it will be easy to pick the items that you need.

» Location is important. Many people put altars in their bedrooms, meditation rooms, guest rooms or spaces that don't have heavy traffic. My husband and I have one in our living room. The important thing is that people know when they see it that this is a sacred space.

» What you put on it is also up to you. It is really nice to have a theme that opens your heart. Some people put candles, fresh flowers, herbs and rocks (nature items), and sculptures of people or things that inspire them. Pictures, crystals and bells are also used quite often. A book is also a nice touch. I put things on my altar that I want to be visible as a blessing for me. I have placed my new CDs and/or books before they were launched. What is important is that your altar doesn't feel cluttered.

» Once you feel good about the altar, bless it. Give thanks that it will be a continuous reminder that you are guided, cared for and deeply supported. Look at it daily and feel free to change it as often as you feel called.

SACRED SPACE EXERCISES

• • • • •

1. Get a Journal and label it DECLUTTERING.

2. Write down your current reality. How do you feel? How are you responding to people and your life?

3. Write down what your life would feel like if you were clear, open and peaceful.

4. Write down the things that you absolutely do not have to do and create a plan to let them go.

5. Put on your calendar time for you (if you don't do this you probably won't find time to nurture you).

6. Get and use a meditation CD that is at least 10 minutes long.

7. Listen to CDs with positive messages in your car.

8. Schedule consistent body work, chiropractic care, manicure/pedicures, etc.

9. Get support from a mentor or coach to help you restructure your business.

10. Create a budget that works for you and allows you to save money.

11. Re-assess each room in your home. Does it feel open and nurturing?

12. Walk into your office. Does it feel good? Does it invite people to engage and feel supported?

Go through each question/section and commit to change anything that does not feel supportive. I recommend that you do one item at a time and check them off when completed. That way you won't feel overwhelmed. It is beneficial to journal feelings and resistance during this process. The clearer you become, the less likely the old behavior will return.

Begin to witness how you feel as each area is cleared. When I did this, I experienced my mind and body feeling more open.

CREATING SACRED SPACE TOOLS

A sacred space can be used to receive, meditate, pray, write, paint or chant. This is a place you pause, get still and learn to listen to your inner voice.

Place pillows, drape fabric, hang a screen or beads in a place that creates the feeling of solitude and stillness. It is a great place to have a yoga mat and to stretch if you have room. A comfortable chair that supports your back is great for meditation.

Set up an altar to bring in the energy of peace and serenity. Plants and flowers are always a nice way to add color and increase oxygen in the space.

Aromatherapy oils and diffusors are a nice way to keep the room fresh. There are also incredible incense fragrances that keep the room smelling great.

Pick pictures of nature, angels, spiritual guides or landscapes that bring harmony to the space.

Have your favorite books, poetry and music that move you into states of peace and contemplation.

Less is more. Keep it simple.

PRAYER FOR CREATING SACRED SPACE

I take this moment to become still. To move into that place within me that knows harmony and peace. I breathe in a peace that passes all understanding and bathes me with unconditional love. I release and let go. I allow the breath to remind me that I am alive and fully supported.

It is from this space that I bless this place. I call in all angels, healers, teachers, guides and avatars assigned to my life. I invite them to participate in this blessing, lifting the vibration of goodness and joy.

I call in abundance, freedom, clarity, comfort, and nurture. These qualities fill the air and the space. I bless every activity here. I bless every prayer and prayer request. I bless every meditation. I bless every item in this room. I know that great expansion and healing takes place here.

Everyone who enters this space feels the energy of love and grace. For this I am thankful and allow it to be.

MIND YOUR WINGS

• • • • •

—Zemirah Jazwierski

Since I was a little girl, I was born to be on stage. I would sit in my playroom, line up Raggedy Ann and Andy, Sock Monkey, Kermit the Frog, Miss Piggy and Cabbage Patch dolls, and teach them all sorts of magically inspiring things.

At age four, my dad taught me to play "Twinkle, Twinkle Little Star" on a touch-tone phone. He connected the phone to speakers so I could debut my skills at the church talent show. My mom taught me piano and, by eight years old, I was belting out "It's A Miracle," playing for the congregation during our Sunday Methodist services.

But then it happened. I realized I could fail. One day, all the wrong notes came out. It was as if I was seeing the piano for the first time! *Then*, in the midst of my blunders, I noticed people were watching. I felt like a fallen angel. I saw looks of embarrassment and confusion on the audience's faces. The more flustered I got, the more wrong notes I played until I stopped completely.

There was a terrible silence. I stood up and bolted off the stage! After that, tears of shame and disappointment drowned my voice and paralyzed me. I didn't play piano on stage again. If asked to speak, my face would tremble and shake and I could hardly remember my words. I shrank painfully into a dark cave of shyness. I was miserable there. Soon, anger and frustration ignited a simmer that would continue for years to come.

Then life sent me a teacher in the form of my daughter, Maddie.

Maddie came into the world larger than life, a born artist. In diapers, she would spend hours drawing microscopic circles on paper. She has an enormous imagination. Once, she fashioned a mermaid tail from flip-flops, duct tape and garden mats and asked me to take her to the athletic club to test the tail's "glide efficiency." Next came the construction of wings. Armed with a self-drawn and designed pattern, she spent days fashioning her creation. There were feathers in every corner of the house, some even hot-glued to the carpet. She soon announced that she'd achieved success. She told me "not to look" as she led me upstairs to her room. Opening the door, I was speechless. There was the most beautiful pair of wings that I could even imagine. Each feather was mindfully placed with love.

I asked, "What are you going to do with the wings?"

"Wear them to school for Halloween!" she answered, looking at me with the *"Seriously, mom,"* expression. As a mom *and* a school psychologist, I kept asking more questions, such as, "How will you sit at your desk?" "Will the teachers care?" "Won't the other students bump into you in the hallway?" But each time she patiently assured me that it was more than possible...in fact, she said, the other students would just have to "mind the wings."

The morning of her angelic flight arrived. She bubbled with excitement as we gingerly placed the wings in the back seat of the car. I pulled up in front of the school. She quickly tied them onto her back. I kissed her cheek as she joyfully marched away. Wiping tears, I snapped some quick pictures as she flew, merging with the throng of students heading towards the school doors. With a last, giant smile she looked back at me and floated out of view into the crowd.

In that moment, I felt my own wings unfurl a little, something in my soul beginning to stir. She had said to "mind the wings." What would happen in my life if I began to mind my own wings? How might I nurture myself back to sharing my gifts? How might I set my voice free? I rolled up my sleeves and tiptoed to the edge of my fear, taking baby steps to start. I started a blog at kidsrelaxation.com, a virtual library where I could share the ideas I was using in schools to help anxious kids. I volunteered to speak at staff meetings and created some Sunday school presentations for my church. It wasn't easy; in fact, the first time I was scheduled to speak, I cancelled and cried all morning, steeped in intense fear. I tried to host a webinar, and my ability to manage the technology completely flopped. But I kept at it, each day asking myself how I might care for my wings.

I saturated my environment with inspirational speakers. I watched TED talks like a scientist taking data. On Sundays at church, not only would I take notes to remember the inspiration, but also to understand the structure of the speech. I began to teach Neurosculpting® classes, a modality that combines brain science with meditation practice. But, most of all, I began to encourage myself from the inside. When I felt fear, I would make lists of my strengths and begin to speak kindly to myself, much as I would speak to a child.

Slowly, in saying *yes*, my wings have expanded. In joining Cynthia James's Mastermind, one of my goals was to polish my speaking skills and to create a transformational speech. I purchased a VIP master speaker day with Cynthia. It was the biggest blessing! She graciously shared her humor, constructive feedback, amazing acting skills, and showed me how to increase stage presence. With her undivided attention to my content and delivery, my inner voice got a giant booster shot of confidence and possibility.

Little pings of fear continue to threaten me and sometimes I still want to hide, but now I've felt and deeply embodied the energy of YES. This energy propels me forward and each moment is now an opportunity to unfurl my wings a little bit more in the direction of my dreams.

Now when I get stuck, I whisper compassionately to myself, "mind the wings." And if I pause long enough, I can feel them unfold.

FINAL THOUGHTS

You are a divinely inspired work of art. You are here to touch the hearts and souls of everyone you meet. Please remember that your withholding your gifts on any level deprives the world of your amazing presence. Step up! Step out! The world is waiting......CHOOSE YOU!

CONTRIBUTORS

* * * * *

Kay Adams is a Licensed Clinical Social Worker, educator, writer, clinician and trainer. Through her work, Kay companions the aging and ill and the families, caregivers and communities touched by and entrusted with their care. Kay believes in bringing authenticity, compassion and humor to her work. She has an extensive background in hospice and in consulting around issues of dementia. Kay has devoted her professional life to being a healing presence and advocate for change. Kay lives in Wheat Ridge, Colorado with her life partner and her precious son, Eli— her very best and most inspirational teacher of all.

Christy Belz's passion lives in the empowerment of you, both personally and professionally. She is gifted at seeing you as a whole person, discerning, uncovering and helping to resolve the underlying issues that can keep you stuck. Specialties include: Life Coaching, Trauma Work including PTSD, WaveMaker and Emotional Energetic Repatterning (EER) Coaching, What Will Set You Freedom Coaching and Executive and Leadership Coaching.

Cheryl Burget has over 20 years of sales experience in the competitive investment management industry. Her passion is teaching entrepreneurs and sales professionals innovative authentic selling strategies. She herself has been a successful entrepreneur since 2007 when she became a facilitator, trainer and speaker inspiring others to discover their own talents, passions and purpose. Cheryl spent eight years as a Senior Master Trainer, training over 1500 Passion Test facilitators representing more than 50 countries worldwide.

Renee Featherstone, an award winning Speaker, Author, and Empowerment Coach, works with individuals and groups to create and maintain "healthy" relationships. With her energetic coaching technique, workshops and seminars, Renee supports her clients to move from the life they live to the life they love. Renee is a co-author of the bestselling book *Living Proof: Celebrating the Gifts That Came Wrapped in Sandpaper,* as well as her e-book *Nine Strategies to Ignite Your Life.* Renee also co-hosts a monthly blog talk radio show, titled *"Into The Light."* Her website is www.IntoTheLightInc.com.

Jean Hendry is a transformation expert focused on supporting you in confidently living the fullest version of yourself by recognizing and owning your unique brilliance. Do you question yourself, wonder if you've got what it takes, and lack confidence? Jean's been there! Her own transformation evolved from many years of self-doubt, low self-esteem and "not good enough-itis" to recognizing and loving her gifts and beauty and confidently sharing them with the world. Her passion is helping women escape those traps and see the beauty in themselves, bringing their brilliant best to the world and having the confidence and the self-esteem to live the full life they deserve. Her website is www. beyourbrilliant.best.

Kellie Christina Jones is committed and dedicated to assisting and supporting clients towards transformation, revelation and healing. She is a powerful intuitive, healer and a gifted and talented freedom coach. Her coaching skills are utilized as a catalyst to support, transform and elevate her clients into shifting their awareness and then taking action.

Pat Jacques is a Certified Freedom Coach adept at identifying blocks and breaking complexity into simplicity. She transformed her early life of violence and abuse to become a pioneer woman racing men's Motocross, earned her college degree, and became a successful woman entrepreneur. Pat listens deeply, making profound connections with her clients to help them achieve authentic, joyful, abundant lives.

Lynda King holds a position as Sr. Manager - Content Strategist in the Employee Success Organization at Salesforce.com, recognized by Forbes as the most innovative company in the world for 4 years straight. Before working at Salesforce, she was Vice President of Global Services at ACI Worldwide, a Global Payments Platform where she led HELP24, the mission-critical technical support operation for 15 years. Over the past 5 years, she has studied life coaching techniques through the Academy for Coaching Excellence and the What Will Set You Free Coaching program offered by Cynthia James Enterprises.

Rev. Kathleen Lenover brings a unique combination of skill sets: 13 years teaching as a Catholic Sister and 33 years as a financial advisor assist her in bringing compassion and understanding as clients experience being truly heard and supported. Rev. Kathleen is a Certified Financial Coach and a licensed minister with Centers for Spiritual Living. She is the founding minister of *Education for Abundant Living*. She has been featured on ABC Home Show, CBS Morning Show, and National Public Radio. She has made numerous appearances on Denver's Channel Nine News, and is a columnist for *Science of Mind Magazine*. Kathleen is author of a white paper entitled, *What Women Want*, and the Forward to a cutting edge book on investing, *The Wealth Solution, Bringing Structure to Your Financial Life*. She resides in Denver, CO.

Angela Sasseville, MA, LPC, is the Executive Director of Flourish Counseling & Coaching in Denver, Colorado and the author of the award-winning book *Families Under Financial Stress*. She's been interviewed about personal fulfillment and relationship issues by PBS, *Parents Magazine* and others.

Lynne Snyder brings over 29 years of experience as a clinical nursing director, managing a large department with over 150 employees. She began her current position at Avista Hospital a year before the hospital opened, helping design the hospital, manage the capital equipment acquisition, recruit and secure physicians, hire all the staff and design the working process, including staffing models, policy, procedures, and marketing.

Liz Wendling is a business consultant, sales expert and emotional intelligence coach. Liz is known for her amazing ability to "close the gap" and take people from where they are now to where they need to be to achieve the results they want and deserve. Her website is www. lizwendling.com

Zemirah Jazwierska, Ed.S. inspires women to live their greatest expression in life by LOOKING DEEPLY within themselves. She nurtures and gently guides clients in realizing their own inherent resiliency. Her products and programs support women in transcending stories of not-enoughness and empowering the courageous steps necessary to manifest dreams. She is passionate about inspiring women to spread their wings for deeper fulfillment in life. She is certified as a Heartmath®, Parenting, and Neurosculpting ® Coach and is the author behind the popular blogs at www.kidsrelaxation.com and www.Shangri-love.com.

ACKNOWLEDGMENTS

* * * * *

To my beloved mother and ancestors. I am so grateful for your presence on the planet. I carry your beauty, strength and courage.

Thank you to my darling husband, Carl, for always seeing me and believing in my talents. Your support is beyond my wildest imaginings.

To my brother, David. You live in my heart.

To my children, Lee and Sharron. Being your mother has been one of the greatest gifts of my life. My heart smiles when I think of you...which is all the time.

DeAnna and Monique, you are blessings to my soul.

To my grandchildren, Randy, Brionne, Mycah, Misah, Talia and Zion. You are so fabulous and I know you are here to do great things.

Jean Hendry, I am so grateful you are partnering with me and daring to leap and grow together.

Beth Oden, I am so grateful for your support in co-creating The Extraordinary Living Foundation. My heart soars when we are with these women.

Betsy Wiersma and Cathy Hawk, thanks for asking me to look at my Big Life.

Dr. James and Debra Rouse, your consistent encouragement helped me get through some tough times and reminded me to focus on health.

Tina Lifford, our late night calls always inspire me to think bigger and ask deeper questions.

Lisa Haas, thanks for helping me navigate the sea of social media.

What Will Set You Free – Freedom Coaches. You are all gifted, amazing and committed. Your support of the women in our programs inspires me.

Lisa Nichols and the Motivating the Masses leadership team. I have grown so much by trusting your brilliance and guidance.

Women Creating Our Futures Mastermind participants and Extraordinary Living Foundation women. I am so honored to support your greatness in the world.

To the contributors to this book, thanks for stepping out and sharing your vulnerable revelations.

Dr. Roger Teel for recognizing my gifts and inviting to me to play bigger in the world.

To my clients, I am consistently amazed at your courage and willingness to be seen.

Thank you administrators and support teams that have supported me bringing my gifts to the world. You have been tremendous blessings.

ABOUT THE AUTHOR

* * * * *

Cynthia James is a transformational specialist guiding people as they make changes for lasting healing in their lives. Ms. James's life was transformed as she transcended a childhood of violence and abuse, and that experience created the foundation for all her programs. Once a working Hollywood actress, Cynthia excels as a speaker, coach, singer and multiple-award winning author of *What Will Set You Free* and *Revealing Your Extraordinary Essence*. Cynthia has coached and supported thousands of people into vibrant living, including taking her workshop *What Will Set You Free* worldwide and to women in prison. Her program *Advanced Awareness Coaching* offers depth, focus and results for high-level business leaders. Cynthia's Extraordinary Living Foundation was selected as a commitment maker by the Clinton Foundation Health Care Initiative

CPSIA information can be obtained
at www.ICGtesting.com
Printed in the USA
FSOW02n0304040816
23356FS